THE ULTIMATE GUIDE TO TECHNICAL ANALYSIS

STEVE BURNS

HOLLY BURNS

© Copyright 2021 Stolly Media, LLC.

All rights reserved. No part of this publication may be reproduced, distributed, or transmitted in any form or by any means without the prior written permission of the publisher, except in the case of brief quotations embodied in critical reviews and certain other noncommercial users permitted by copyright law.

The historical chart patterns in this book were created by Jake Wujastyk (@Trendspider_J), founding team member at **TrendSpider.com**

DISCLAIMER

This book is meant to be informational and shouldn't be used as trading advice. All traders should gather information from multiple sources, and create their own trading systems. Always consult a registered investment advisor before conducting trades. The authors make no guarantees related to the claims contained herein. Please trade responsibly.

FOREWORD

Most of us get into trading with preconceived ideas about markets, prices, asset classes, even charting software. Everyone has an opinion about everything... Everyone, except Steve. He is able to get down to the facts, removing all room for opinion, sharing only the most important and applicable information for the indicators and analysis strategies he explains throughout this book.
Once again, Steve is able to deliver a concise and powerful message through real tactics and real experience. Out of all the books Steve has written, this one is a stand-out.
With day trading becoming increasingly popular, this is the perfect time for this book. We all know how difficult it can be when searching for reliable information in the ever-crowded internet space that we operate in today.
Steve has a unique way of explaining technical indicators that cut through any form of vagueness. If I had to, I would put this book ahead of Steve Nisson's 'Beyond Candlesticks', Because Burns makes it so much more digestible and relatable.
I've been active in the markets for 6 years, almost every single day. I've seen and heard about every indicator in the world... or so I

thought. This book surprised me, sharing information about indicators I had never heard of.

In this book, Steve is able to tastefully and tactfully layout technical analysis, the art of reading a chart. Not only does Steve open our eyes to new forms of analysis, but he backs up their history with real chart examples throughout. This book goes beyond just reiterating dictionary definitions of technical indicators, it dives into their history and attaches deeper meaning to the power they possess.

Steve has graced us yet again.
You're going to love this book.
Thank you, Steve.

Austin Silver
Co-Owner, Head Of Trading & Education at ASFX
www.asfx.biz

1
WHAT IS TECHNICAL ANALYSIS?

Technical analysis is a process that evaluates historical price action on charts to identify trading signals with an edge. Technical analysis is a different school of thought than fundamental analysis. While technical analysis focuses on price action, chart patterns, and the current trend, fundamental analysis focuses on a company's financials like earnings, book value and cash flow. Fundamental analysis looks for trends in earnings and sales to project future stock prices. Fundamental analysis projects the potential future value of the underlying company a stock represents, or the intrinsic value of a commodity or currency based on the trends supply and demand in the economy.

There are many technical indicators that attempt to measure the rate of change in price action, like the Relative Strength indicator (RSI). Other indicators, like moving averages, are designed to filter the volatility of price action to quantify trends. Other indicators attempt to quantify a probable trading range like Bollinger Bands®.

Technical indicators are not crystal balls that predict the future, nor are they the holy grail of trading. Market price action changes from trends to price ranges, and from low volatility to high volatility.

Technical indicators are good for building a system that can measure risk on each trade, and as trading tools to quantify the best entries and exits. These indicators are also helpful for identifying your risk and reward through technical stop losses, and for projecting potential rewards based on key technical price levels.

In this book, we will be looking at types of technical indicators and how to use them in trading. We will also look at price action and how it can create patterns of support and resistance on a chart before breaking out into a new trend. The goal of this book is to show you how to use technical analysis to identify, quantify and trade momentum, volatility and trends through the filter of volume. Here are some basic examples.

- Bollinger Bands® are a technical trading tool that are best used in range-bound markets to measure support and resistance levels, when price gets extended from a medium-term moving average like the 20-day moving average.
- Relative Strength Index (RSI) is for finding good risk / reward ratios during overbought (70 RSI) or oversold (30 RSI) conditions. The RSI can work in both trends and range-bound markets, but it doesn't work when a market price goes into a parabolic trend.
- The Moving Average Convergence/Divergence (MACD) is a useful tool for measuring swings in price up and down on charts.
- Long-term moving averages like the 200-day can be used for identifying long term trends.
- Short-term moving averages like the 5-day and the 10-day are for trading short term swings that have momentum.
- The Average True Range (ATR) measures the trend of volatility of the price range.

Technical analysis can be used to identify levels of price support and resistance, the direction of a current trend, momentum or volatility. Technical indicators are simply trading tools, the profits come from how well a trader uses them to build a price action trading system that fits their time frame, risk tolerance and return goals. Technical analysis without a quantified trading system is unlikely to yield profitable results because traders need a repeatable edge and proper position sizing to make money in the markets. Technical indicators are powerful tools traders can use to construct a successful and profitable price action strategy.

2

TECHNICAL ANALYSIS VS. FUNDAMENTAL ANALYSIS

Before we look at what technical analysis is, let's first see what it is not. Technical analysis is the trading of price action, while fundamental analysis is the trading of value. These are vastly different things. First, we'll examine fundamental analysis.

Fundamental analysis is a method of valuing how much an investment is worth based on quantifying its intrinsic value, both in the present and the future. Company stocks are valued for their businesses, which include their assets, cash flow, growth potential, intellectual property and anything of value that it owns or controls.

Fundamental analysis seeks to make timing decisions on when to buy and sell by quantifying the value of a company based on the variance between the current stock price and the total value of the underlying company. A fundamental investor wants a competitive price on the current value of a company, believing that the stock price will go up more in the future as the true value is priced in over time.

A fundamental investor can look to buy a stock with high future growth potential that is not currently priced in accurately or look to buy a good company at a great price when a low stock price is seen as a good value.

While a current stock value is an investor's opinion, the goal of the fundamental investor is to evaluate the sales and earnings trend of a company in relation to its current price. Fundamental analysis can be used in all financial markets like stocks, currencies, commodities, real estate and precious metals, because they all have underlying fundamental value. Anything that will affect the intrinsic value of an asset is measured in fundamental analysis.

Fundamental analysis looks at stocks the same way they would a business, evaluating price, value, growth and cash flow. Fundamental analysis quantifies entries based on value versus price. It quantifies exits when the fundamentals of the investment have permanently changed, or the price far exceeds the current or future value of a stock or asset.

Technical analysis focuses only on price action and volume. The best use of technical analysis is not the prediction of future price. Instead, it should be used to identify the path of least resistance, quantify the probabilities of what will happen next and to identify a price level of entry for a good risk/reward ratio.

Pure price action is primarily used as an indicator of how traders and investors have acted around price levels previously and how they may make buying and selling decisions in the future. Technical indicators are derivatives of price action and are also used to measure and quantify trends, overbought/oversold levels, momentum, divergences, deviations from the mean and trading ranges.

Technical analysts, chartists and market technicians can use several types of charts to add more visual dimensions to visual price action like candlesticks, bar charts, line charts, point and figure charts and raindrop charts.

Technical trading focuses on the price action in chart patterns, trends, support and resistance levels. It also focuses on where the volume occurs on a chart to identify the type of market environment. It's also used to create price action signals for both trade entries and exits on a chart.

The goal of a technical trader should be to create a price action trading system with an edge that has a positive expectancy based on the average win versus the average loss. Profitability can be accomplished through a high win rate if losses are kept small, or with a lower win rate if it has a good risk/reward ratio. This allows the bigger wins to pay for all the small losing trades, with money left over for profits.

Technical analysis doesn't consider the fundamentals when trading a stock or asset as the focus is on price action. However, fundamental analysis can be considered in the process of building a watchlist so the trader can choose what stocks or assets to trade based on good fundamentals. A trader can then decide when to trade them based on technical price action.

A trader or investor can choose to focus on either fundamental or technical analysis or a combination of both; both have strengths that can improve profitability. Fundamentals can tell you what to buy and technical analysis can tell you when to buy and sell it.

- Fundamentals = Current and future value
- Price = Current buying and selling reality

3

DOES TECHNICAL ANALYSIS WORK?

Many people believe technical analysis is complete nonsense. How can someone make money on lines and patterns on a price chart? In the past, people have jumped to conclusions and assumed that there are no rich technical analysts. Many new traders doubt technical analysis, largely due to their inexperience trading and backtesting systems.

Academics doubt technical analysis despite its solid process, including creating a proper watchlist, positions sizing, trade management, profit factor, volatility filters, the importance of an edge and trading with discipline. However, two authors did the necessary research to prove that technical analysis not only works but has made many traders a lot of money.

Books by Michael Covel and Jack Schwager document how technical traders used price action over decades to consistently get rich. These trader's accounts are not opinion, they are fact. Saying that technical traders can't make money is like saying that It's impossible to make money as a professional athlete while ignoring all the rich athletes playing professional sports.

There are two types of technical analysis.

- Predictive technical analysis- traders attempt to project what will happen next in price movement based on a current chart pattern. They look for the clues of volume, trendlines and the levels of support and resistance to project the probabilities of future price movement.
- Reactive technical analysis- a trader's entries and exits are based on current price signals that backtest as profitable by creating good risk/reward ratios. Their quantified price signals indicate when to get in for a good probability of success and when to get out with a small loss if a trade is a loser, or when to lock in a profit if the trade is a winner.

The best use of both types of technical analysis is to create good risk/reward ratios on entry. This tells you where to get out for a small loss if the trade doesn't work out, and the potential magnitude of the win if the trade is a winner. The value of all types of technical analysis is in creating good risk/reward ratios by identifying levels of potential risk versus levels of potential reward.

In his Market Wizard Book Series, Jack Schwager detailed different traders using both predictive and reactive technical analysis to make a lot of money over extended periods of time. Likewise, Michael Covel's Trend Following book discussed the millionaire and billionaire traders that used reactive technical analysis to effectively follow market trends and become wealthy.

Technical Analysis alone is meaningless outside the parameters of a complete trading system. A trader needs proper position sizing, a trading watchlist, a strategy with an edge and the discipline and perseverance to stick to their trading rules. This discipline is what makes it possible for a trader to allow their edge to play out over time and lead to profitability.

People's opinions about whether technical analysis works don't matter. The fact is that technical analysis has worked for many and if they did it, others can follow the same process.

4

SUPPLY AND DEMAND

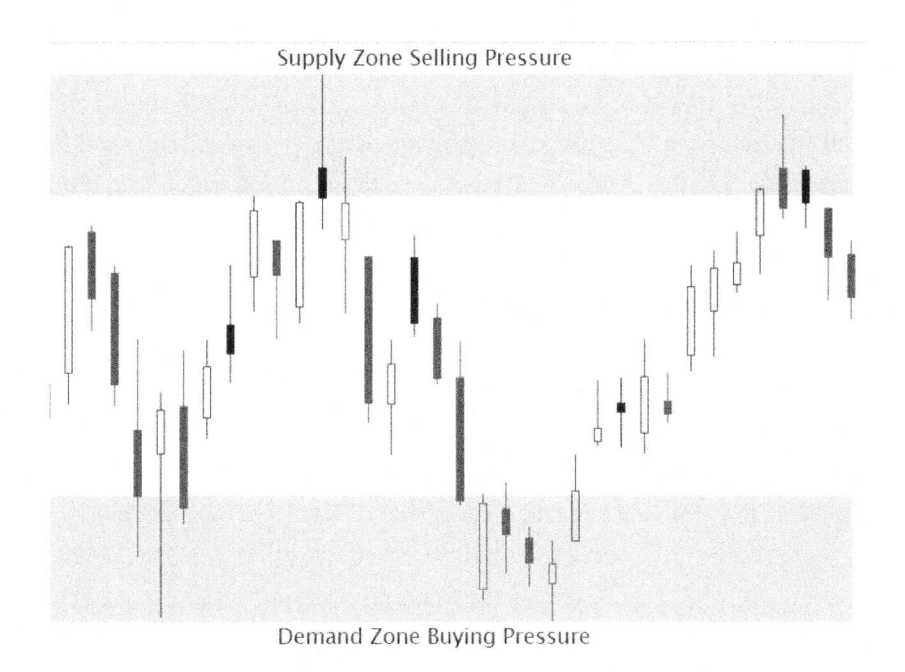

*S*upply creates resistance on a chart, demand creates the support.

. . .

How do you identify supply and demand zones on a chart?

Areas of supply for a market at higher price levels is what creates resistance. An area of supply is a price zone where many traders and investors are holding a stock and willing to sell it and exit their position. Overhead resistance is created when people sell to lock in their gains at their profit target levels. A supply level can also be created when people want to get back to even after being in a losing trade or investment, and the price rallies back to where they bought it. Supply is the inventory people are holding for a market at a price level, and they want to unload it when given the opportunity.

Areas of demand for a market can be at lower price levels that create support. An area of demand is a price zone where many traders and investors want to buy a market when price gets back to that level. Lower price levels of support are created when people have been waiting to buy a market at a lower price when it returns to that point. This could be an old area trading at a lower price, an oversold reading on a chart or a key moving average support. Demand is the area of support where buy orders are set because people think it's a chance to get a value price with a good risk/reward ratio on entry. The demand area for buyers is created by the traders and investors that believe in buying low now and selling high later.

There can be a correlation with volume and support and resistance zones. The price that markets trade can create areas of interest that illustrate traders and investors are making transactions.

A price zone with a large volume of buyers trying to get into a breakout that fails can create a lot of buyers that become trapped at higher prices in a descending chart. These trapped buyers can create a future supply and resistance zone. They are happy to exit to get out at even when given another chance with a rally back to the failed breakout area.

An old support area that had high demand in volume may create a price zone where many stop losses are set. A lot of volume at an old area of support can set the stage for a downward move to new lower prices if the key support area is lost with no demand from new buyers. Large drops in price can occur when a significant group of stop losses are triggered simultaneously at an obvious level of support on a chart.

Look for price zones of meaning that set the highs or the lows on a chart without being broken to the upside or downside over a period of time.

A supply zone is a price level where current holders of a market are located and are willing to sell when price reaches that area. A demand zone is a price level where traders and investors on the sidelines are willing to step in and buy when prices get that low.

A supply zone is the price levels on a chart where the sellers are located, while the demand zone are the price levels on a chart where the buyers are located. Technical analysis can help you locate the highest probability areas on a chart where the buyers or sellers are waiting to enter or exit their positions.

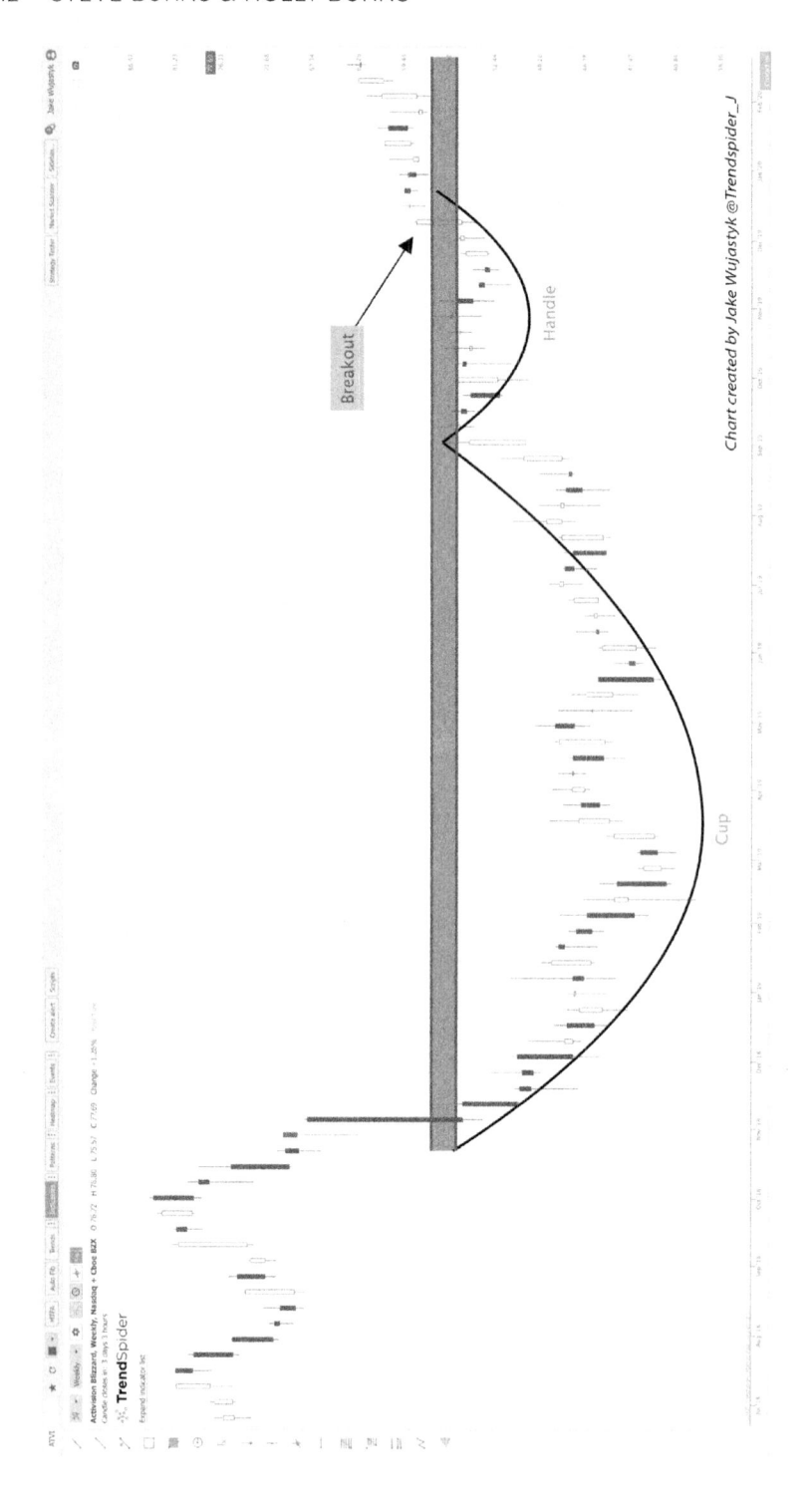

5

SUPPORT AND RESISTANCE

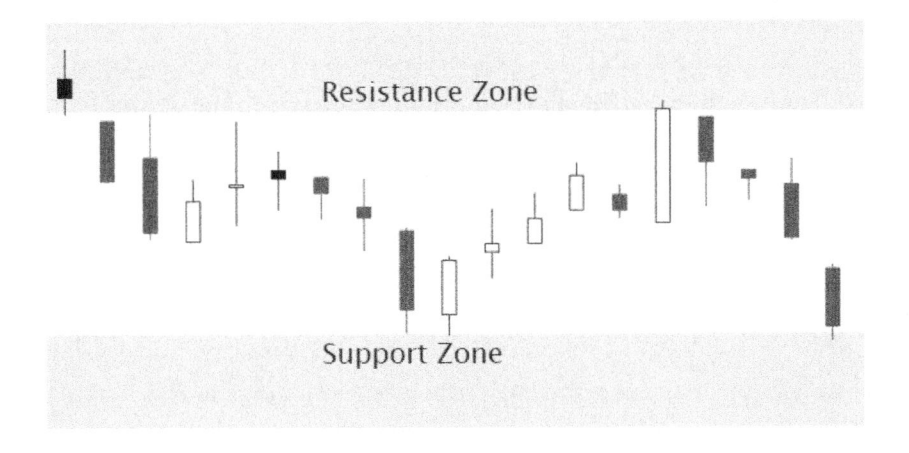

Resistance Zone

Support Zone

Support and resistance price levels can show where buyers and sellers are located at different price levels on a chart. Support is created when buyers keep price from going lower at a certain level on a chart. Resistance is created at a price where the sellers can't be overcome by buyers at a price level. The price levels that buyers and sellers are willing to enter and exit a trade at is what creates support and resistance on a chart.

Support and resistance on a chart can be horizontal or vertical. Support and resistance are a way to measure and quantify whether a chart is currently in an uptrend, downtrend or going sideways in your time frame. Horizontal support and resistance around a price area repeatedly show sideways price action on a chart. Support and resistance ascending to higher-highs and higher low-price levels indicate that a price is in an uptrend. Support and resistance descending to lower highs and lower low-price levels shows that a price is in a downtrend.

A repeated lower price level that is revisited but has dip buying where the chart stops descending is considered the *chart support*. A repeated higher price level that is revisited but has profit taking and the chart stops going higher due to selling pressure in an area is considered the chart resistance.

Horizontal support and resistance areas show that a chart is trading in a price range. This condition remains until either support is broken to the downside or resistance is broken to the upside, opening the possibility for a new trend to emerge.

Support and resistance levels are not an exact price to watch, rather it's a zone of prices. A valid area of support or resistance is indicated when there are repeated tests of the upside or downside of a price area. The longer a chart trades in a price range the more valid the areas become. Also, the longer the price range the more powerful the eventual breakout can be.

A break below support or a break above resistance could signal the end of the current trading range. This could lead to either more volatility outside the current range, a new price range, or a new trend.

Many times, a trader will see the old resistance become the new support, or the old support become the new resistance, as people buy or sell at a second opportunity at a previous key price level.

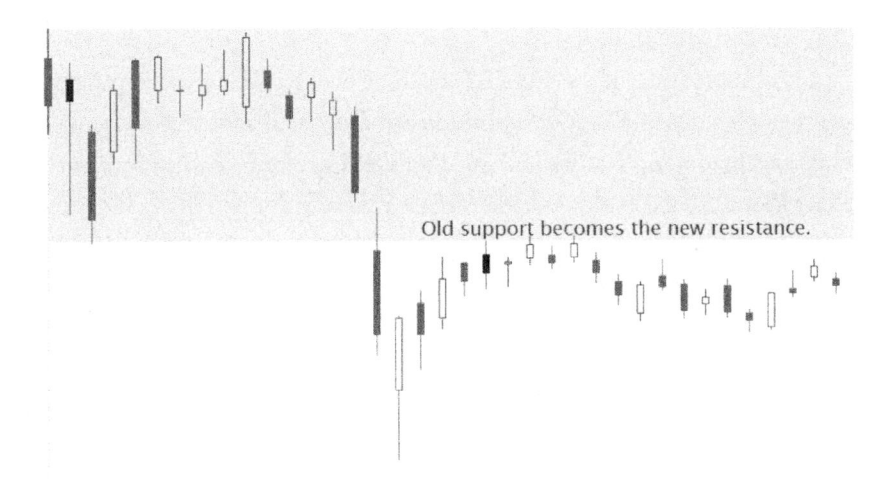

Horizontal support and resistance zones on a chart are visual ways to quantify, identify and track the trend on a chart by identifying price levels of interest on a chart.

Support and resistance zones on a chart can also be vertical, indicating buying and selling interest at price levels identified by ascending or descending moving averages or trendlines.

Ascending support areas happen during uptrends as traders buy dips and pullbacks to a key short-term moving average or vertical trendline. Ascending resistance areas happen during uptrends as traders sell rallies and into moves higher at a key overhead vertical trendline.

Descending resistance areas happen during downtrends as traders sell into rallies back to a key short-term moving average or a vertical trendline above overall price action. Descending support areas happen during downtrends as traders buy dips during sell offs into moves lower to a key vertical trendline of support.

Support price levels are created when buyers decide at what price level they will buy the dip. Charts stop descending when enough buyers show up at a price level and can overcome the selling pressure on the chart and stop the move lower. Resistance price levels are created when sellers decide at what price level they will sell into a rally on a chart, and then they overcome the buying pressure, stopping a move any higher.

Technical indicators can add another level for observing potential support and resistance levels on a chart. The readings of these indicators can give signals to buyers and sellers on when to show up on a chart based on oversold, overbought or momentum signals. These are the principles in technical analysis that create horizontal and vertical resistance and support zones on charts.

6

TRENDLINES

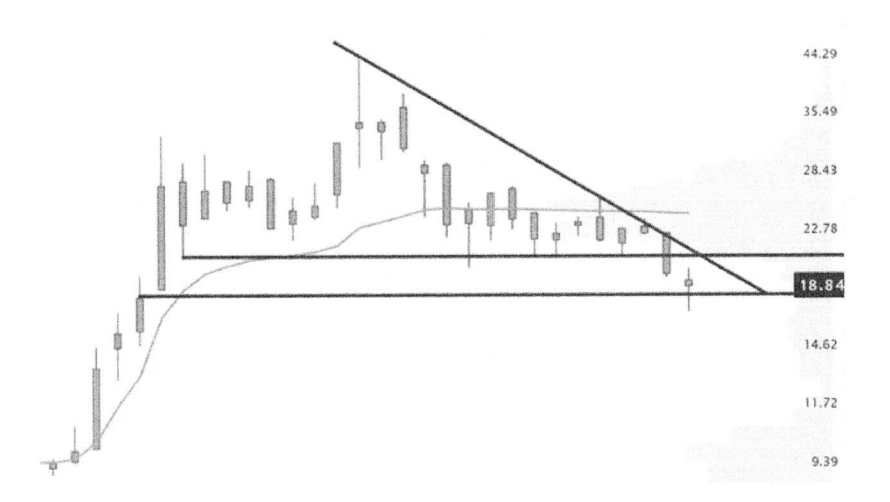

Trendlines are the identifiers and connectors of resistance and support in chart patterns. They measure and quantify the path of least resistance for a chart in your time frame. Trendlines are identifiers of the trend in your trading time frame.

Vertical trendlines must be drawn from left to right to identify one of the following:

A trend of higher highs signals an uptrend. A trend of higher lows shows support in an uptrend.

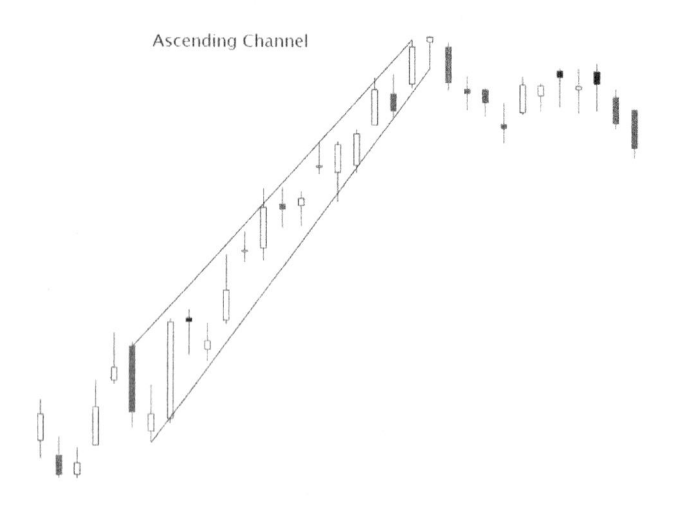

A trend of lower lows signals a downtrend. A trend of lower highs shows resistance in a downtrend.

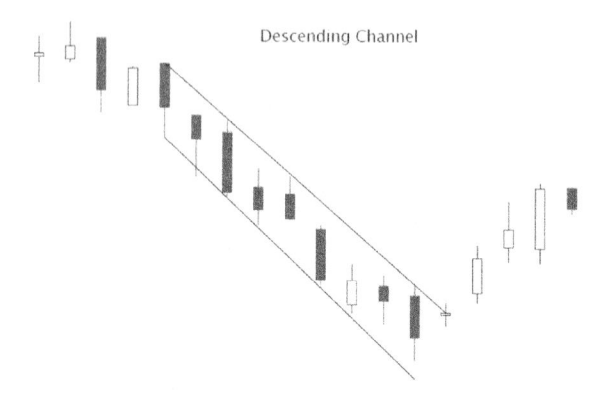

Horizontal trendlines must be drawn straight from left to right to identify price levels of resistance based on unbroken, repeating high prices. Horizontal trendlines can also show levels of support based on repeating lows that hold.

Horizontal Resistance Trend Line

Horizontal Support Trend Line

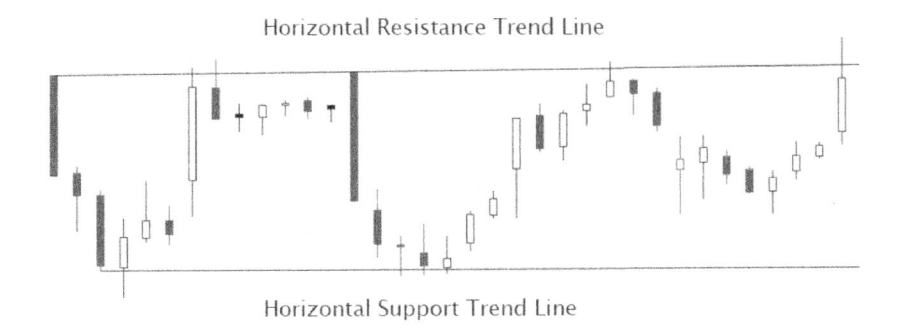

Trendlines can connect short-term time frames end of period prices or the full range of prices. The wicks represent intra-day prices that were outside the open or the close on candlestick charts. Some traders use the end of period prices and others connect the candle wicks, and both are viable options for trendlines.

Trendlines should connect at least two price levels in a direct path to be considered viable. The more connections that they make the more meaningful it is. Trendlines must be updated to ensure a trend is still in place. A trader should see a connection of the lines creating a trend of prices in their trading time frame.

A breakout of price through a trendline can indicate the beginning of a change in trend, or even a new market environment. A market could go from an uptrend or downtrend to a sideways range as your trendline breaks or reverse completely and move in the opposite direction.

Trendlines are visual ways to measure, identify and track the trends on a chart by connecting vertical or horizontal support and resistance on a chart.

Price channels can be up, down or sideways. There are uptrend, downtrend and range-bound price channels. A trading channel can be vertical or horizontal and is defined by trendlines. Vertical ascending uptrend channels are defined by parallel higher highs and higher lows.

Vertical downtrend channels are defined by parallel lower highs and lower lows. Horizontal descending trendlines are defined by parallel lines that have price resistance around the same area of a high price level and price support around a similar lower area of price.

Resistance lines in a chart pattern indicate where buyers are absent at higher prices and where selling pressure at those prices set in.

Support lines on a chart pattern are where buyers step in to buy at a price level to prevent prices from going lower, stopping the selling pressure.

When a horizontal price channel is broken higher, often the old resistance becomes the new support. Likewise, when a horizontal price channel is broken lower, the old support becomes the new resistance.

Channels are for identifying where buyers and sellers are located. Trendlines are best used for giving a wider view of the trend on a chart.

Momentum and trend signals are given when a well-defined price channel is broken.

Another name for a horizontal price chart pattern is a rectangle chart pattern. The breakout of the range in either direction can be the signal to enter a trade in the direction of the break.

Trendlines are some of the most basic technical indicators because they first quantify the type of price action on a chart, uptrend, downtrend or sideways. Trendlines are indicators that quickly show the trader the path of least resistance, whether it is up, down or sideways. Trendlines are a good place to start with basic technical analysis on a chart.

Lower trendline using the body of the candlesticks as support.

THE ULTIMATE GUIDE TO TECHNICAL ANALYSIS   21

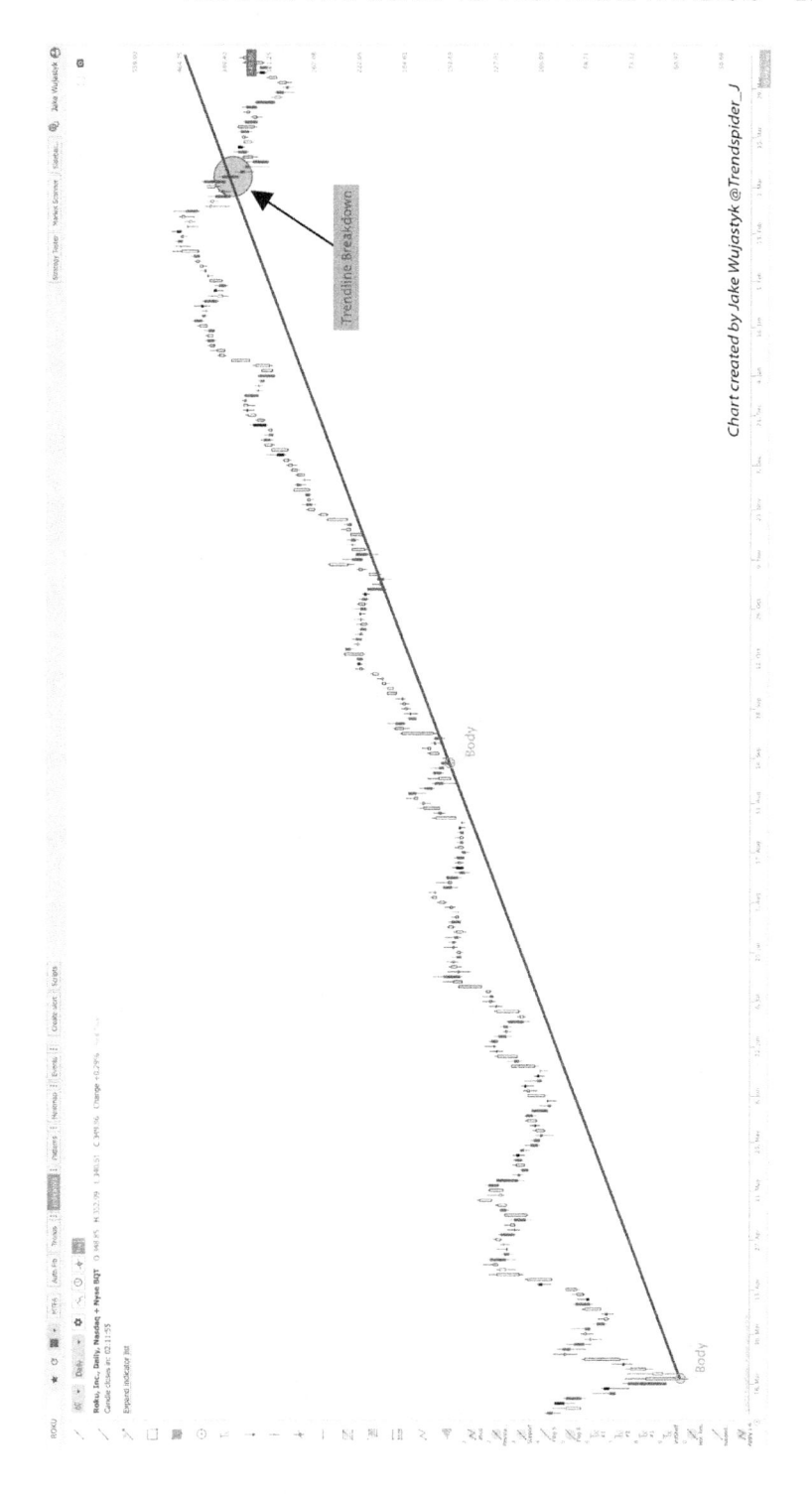

Lower trendline using the wicks of the candlesticks as support.

THE ULTIMATE GUIDE TO TECHNICAL ANALYSIS 23

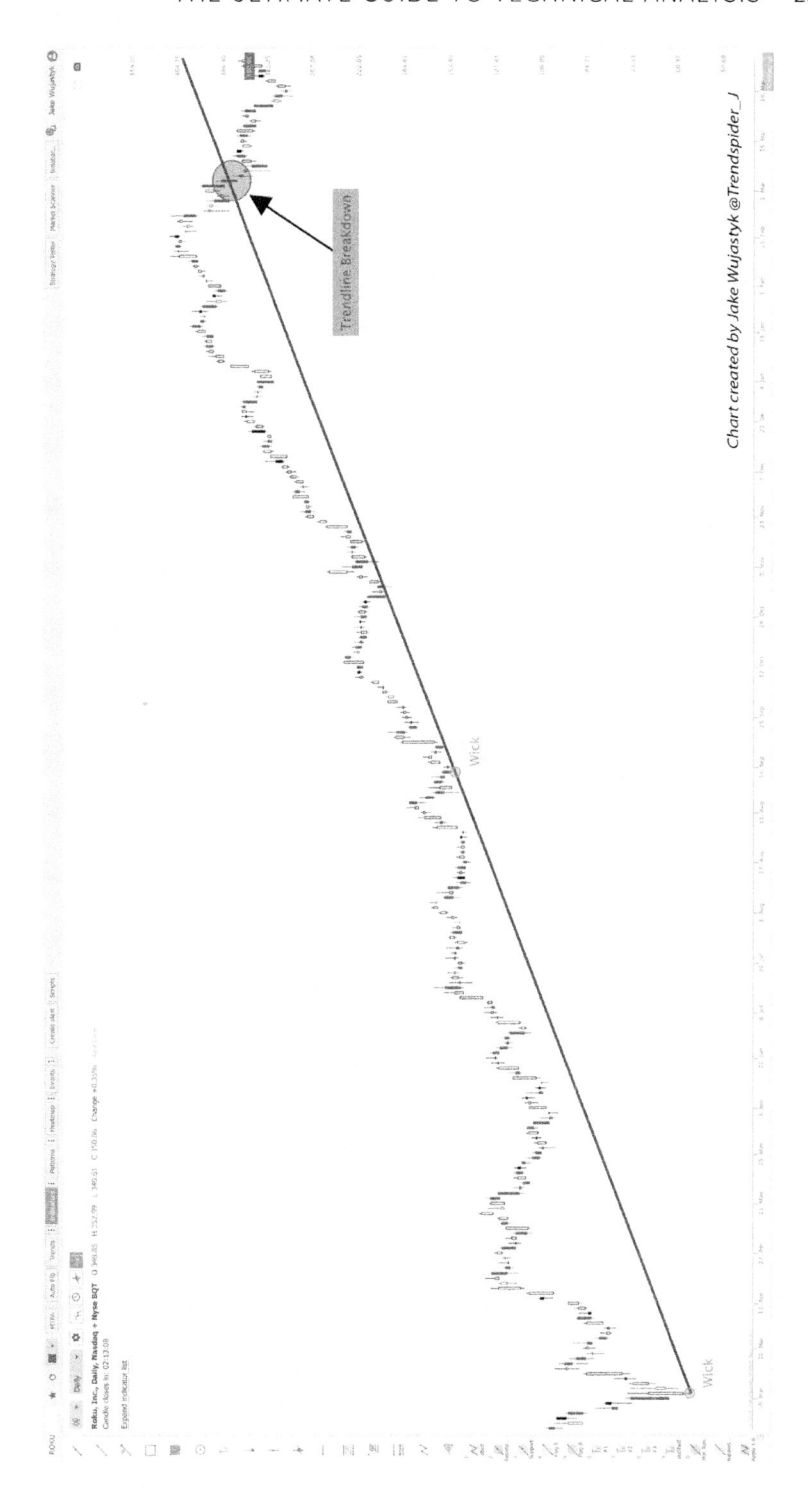

7

GAPS

Gap up in price

A breakaway gap is a chart pattern in technical analysis that shows a large opening gap in price above the previous day's closing price. The gap in price action on the chart is where no trading took place between buyers and sellers. A breakaway gap to the upside must break above previous resistance while a breakaway gap to the downside must break below the previous support.

The price action in this pattern breaks away from the support or resistance zone in a chart via a gap on the next open instead of during intraday movement. To capture a breakaway gap, a trader usually holds overnight to have a position in place prior to the price jump. A breakaway gap is one of the biggest momentum signals indicating the beginning of a new trend or continuation of a trend already taking place. This move must happen as a breakout of a trading range to be valid, and a break to all-time highs or all-time lows is the strongest signal of a new trend beginning.

A breakaway gap is a breakout momentum signal showing the high probability of a continuation in the direction of the gap. Most breakaway gaps ignore overbought or oversold indicators and go parabolic in one direction. Most of the time, this type of gap in a stock happens after an earnings report or on breaking news. Other types of gap moves are runaway gaps that come before a big move, exhaustion gaps at the end of an uptrend and ordinary price gaps.

One way to trade bullish breakaway gaps to the upside:

- Bullish breakaway gaps could be bought at the open for a potential quick gain as momentum continues but there is still a high possibility that the gap could collapse. An early morning gap that fails can be a volatile reversal, but the odds are that the right leading stock will continue in the direction of the gap for at least the rest of the day. Better odds for an entry working are if a trader waits for the gap to hold for the first hour of trading and then enters. There may be a better entry on a pullback to avoid being caught if the gap fails and price collapses. Buying breakaway gaps at the end of the day provide the highest probability that it's a gap and go and not a gap and crap.
- A gap in price that doesn't get filled in the first hour of the trading day tends to keep going in the direction of the gap, most of the time for the remainder of the day.
- Gaps in charts with historical high volatility don't tend to

hold up and trend as well as a gap out of a clean price base.
- A gap above all-time highs has a better chance of success than a random one inside an old price range on the chart where buyers are trapped at higher prices and want to get back out at even.
- A gap to new all-time highs is powerful as all holders are now in a profit and tend to let their profits run. This is the blue-sky breakout that can be powerful, with no stop losses to be triggered and the only selling pressure coming from profit taking.
- Short sellers caught with a position in breakaway gaps to the upside can be additional buyers pushing the trends higher as they are forced to buy to cover their short positions.
- A good place to set a stop loss when buying a gap is under the lowest price of the gap up day. Price shouldn't fall below that level if it's going to continue to trend higher. Using an end of day stop gives you better odds of not being stopped out if it just dips there temporarily.
- If the low of the day holds and a trend begins over multiple days, the trailing stop can be moved to the 10-day moving average, and then the 5-day moving average to lock in profits on a reversal while letting the trend continue. On a very volatile stock, some traders use the 20-day moving average as a trailing stop, so they aren't shaken out of a large winning trade.
- Sometimes, a momentum growth stock that gaps up and trends doesn't have long-term resistance and it just pauses between higher highs. Overbought indicators may not work in momentum growth stocks under heavy accumulation by money managers as the chart goes parabolic. RSI extremes can go farther than expected.
- When caught on the wrong side of a breakaway gap

against a short position, it's usually best to exit in the first 30 minutes. If the gap holds and makes higher highs early in the trading day, it typically gets worse as the day goes on.
- Gaps have a way of leaving many retail traders on the sidelines because they don't want to chase the move. Some of the biggest winning trades can be buying into breakaway gap ups with the right position sizing and letting the winner run.

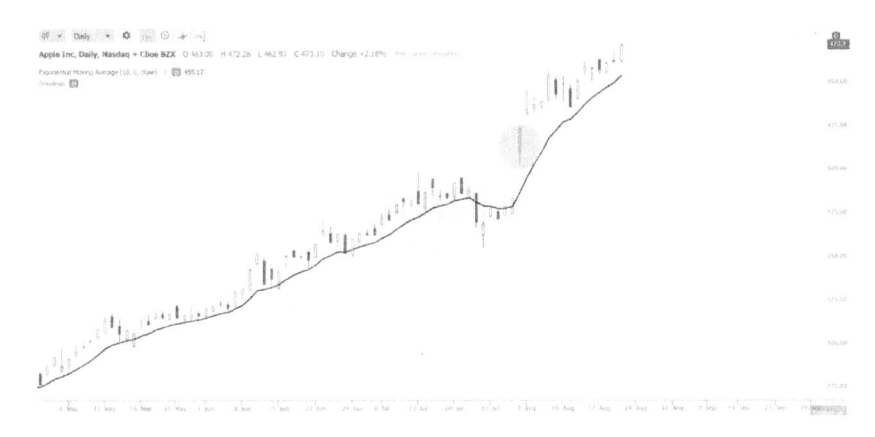

Chart Courtesy of TrendSpider.com

An exhaustion gap is a bearish reversal signal on a chart that occurs after a sharp move higher. It occurs near a high in price on a chart when a space forms between a closing price and the next opening price. This pattern generally has the most meaning on a daily chart. This pattern is formed after a gap up but then a sharp fall in prices from the gap highs showing a quick shift of control from buyers to sellers. A so-called, gap and crap, happens when a chart is bid down in price from the beginning of the daily candle after the gap fails to hold. This is a bearish indicator of a move lower based on technical analysis.

The exhaustion gap signal shows that the supply and demand for the stock has shifted to selling pressure. The probabilities shift to prices going lower after the gap up fails. The probability of even lower prices increases as the candle moves lower through the gap in price area.

- This signal shows a large shift in momentum from going up to going down quickly.
- The exhaustion gap should happen on higher-than-normal volume for stronger confirmation.
- This chart pattern is called an exhaustion gap as it visually shows that buyers are tired of buying at higher prices. They're so exhausted that they can't hold prices up, allowing sellers to take over with a gap down and push the chart much lower.
- An exhaustion gap should be preceded with several days, weeks or even months of an uptrend in prices making new highs.
- A large gap between the closing price of the previous day and the opening price of the current day is the primary visual signal for this pattern.

An exhaustion gap lower in price is a warning to close long positions on the open as well as a new potential short sell signal for positions betting on lower prices. This is an extremely bearish signal showing an absence of buyers in the price gap, as well as a complete change in an upward trend on a chart.

THE ULTIMATE GUIDE TO TECHNICAL ANALYSIS   29

Chart Courtesy of TrendSpider.com

Gaps show that there were no buyers and sellers connecting at price levels on a chart. Gaps happen mostly when news comes out that instantly changes perceived value to much higher or lower prices than they were previously trading. As the news event is instantly priced in by buyers and sellers, a void is left in the chart. Fear and greed can also come into play and causes extreme moves beyond what is rational.

The common saying by traders is that *Gaps always get filled, Charts hate gaps* and *Mind the gap*. A gap on a chart is filled when the price action moves back through the open gap area with missing transactions. Price must retrace all the way to the closing price of the previous day before the gap. Price is technically filled when it returns to the place it was before the gap day. If price moves inside the gap area but doesn't move all the way through it, it's called a partial gap fill.

Gaps can give strong technical signals of momentum, trend continuation or a reversal signal depending on when they happen on a chart.

- A gap up out of a price base to all-time highs can be a new strong momentum signal to the upside.

- A gap down out of a price base to new all-time lows can be a new strong momentum signal to the downside.
- During a trend in price, a gap in the direction of the current move can be a signal of a continuation of the trend already in place.
- A trend in a price gap against the direction of the current move can be a signal of the trend reversing.
- If a gap in the opening price doesn't fill in the first hour of trading it tends to go in the direction of the gap for the rest of the trading day.

Gaps do eventually fill, but it can happen after a strong move or trend takes place and may take a long time for the market to change direction. The path of least resistance is generally in the direction of the gap in price action. There are few technical signals stronger than a gap in price, the bigger the gap the stronger the signal.

THE ULTIMATE GUIDE TO TECHNICAL ANALYSIS   31

Gap in price action

Gap fill in price action

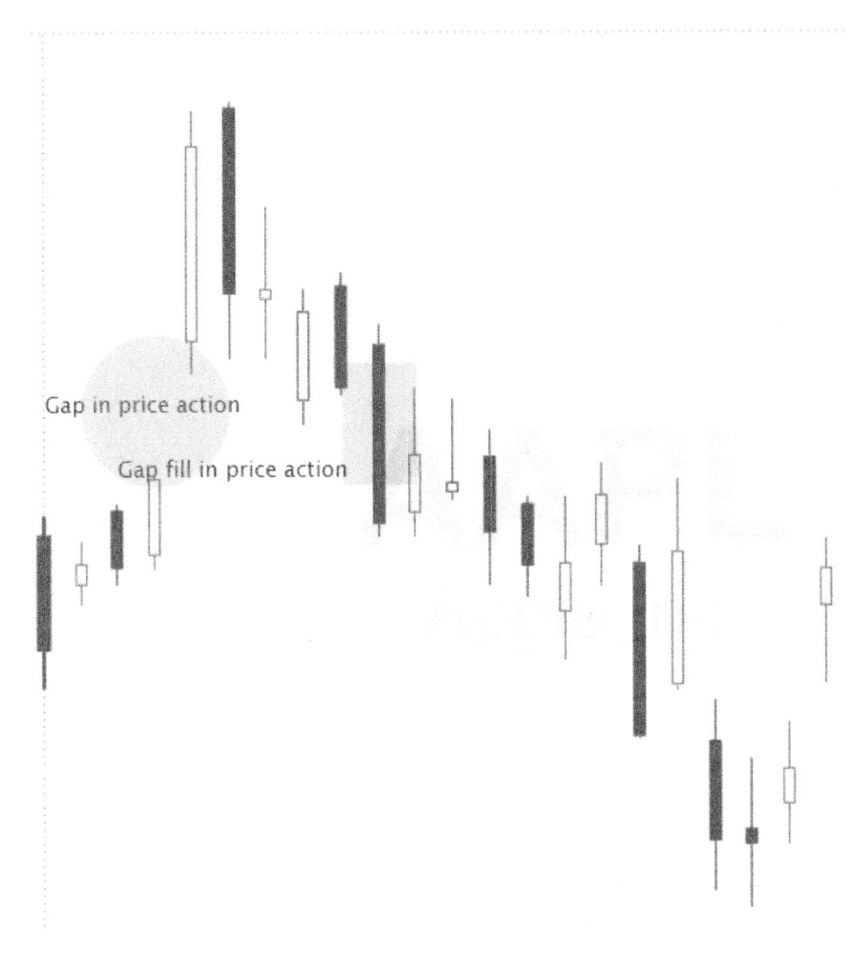

Chart Courtesy of TrendSpider.com

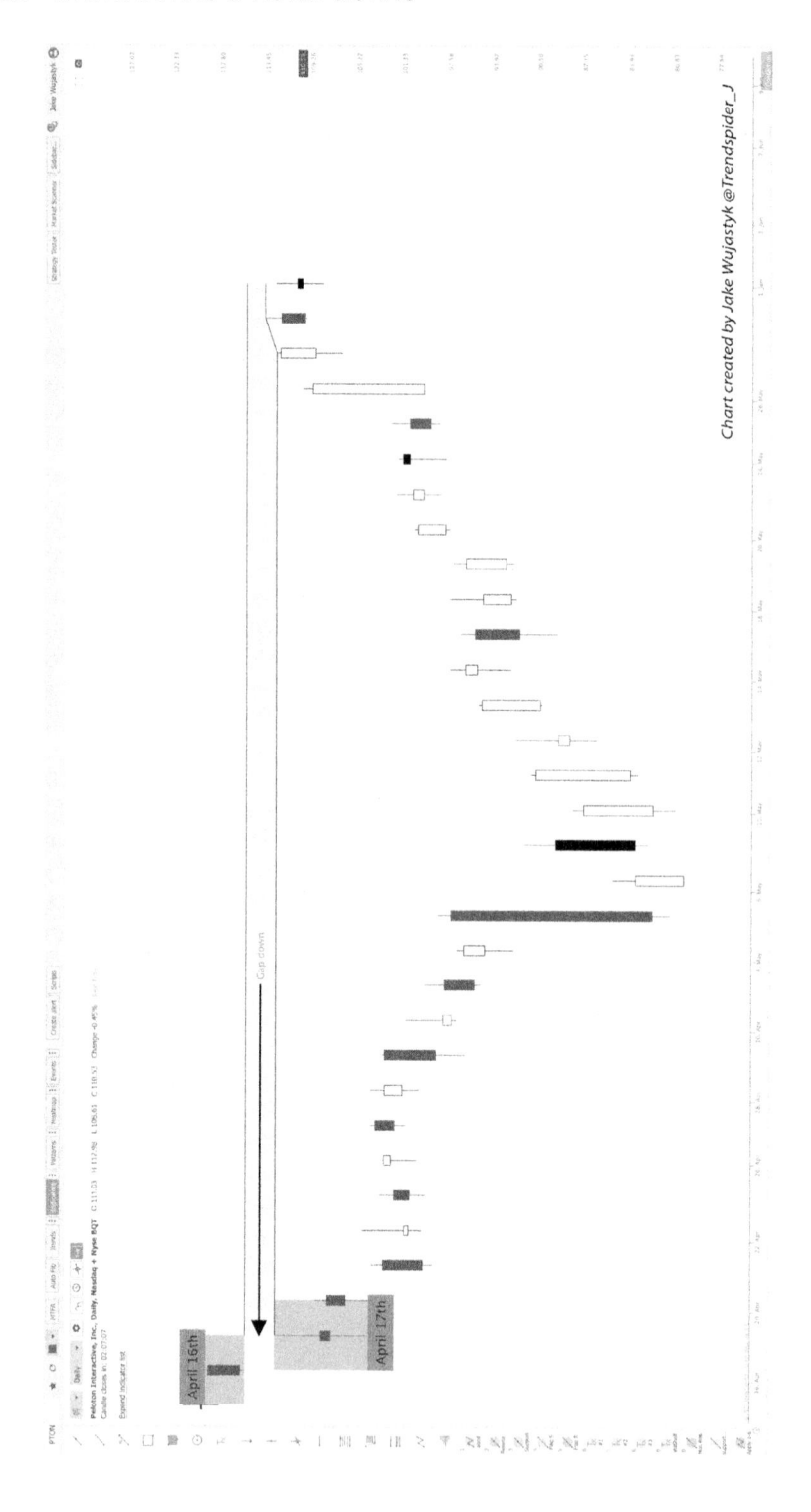

8

BREAKOUTS

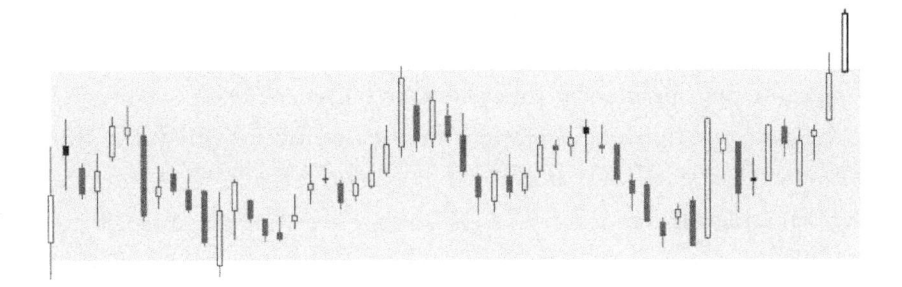

The flat top breakout chart pattern gets its name from the top of the chart being flat, as sellers and buyers have met and agreed at the key resistance level. Once trades take place above that flat upper resistance level, it's considered a breakout above that level.

Flat top breakout trading is used by many momentum traders and trend followers to enter a long position in a market that has broken above resistance out of a long-term price trading range. Some times traders also use a flat top breakout on the intraday chart to trade the quick momentum that can happen after price reaches a new high price on the day.

A flat top breakout can look like a flat base pattern, but the difference is the flat top happens at the highs of resistance, while a flat base can happen inside a long-term trading range and doesn't press new highs in price.

The flat top breakout pattern on top growth stocks can see large movements to the upside after being broken. In this type of a breakout, buyers and sellers have worked through supply in the trading range. When there are no more shares to buy under the resistance price to meet the demand, a chart will make higher prices above that resistance level.

A breakout to new all-time highs in price can gain momentum and begin a new trend. In this pattern, the old resistance can become the new support on pullbacks, as people who missed the first breakout will buy that price again if given a second chance. When all holders have a profit at the highs, there tends to be less selling pressure and price can start moving higher.

Trend followers and momentum traders like to stay on the right side of the trend, and this type of a breakout on a daily chart is a signal for the direction of the next move. Day traders want a quick price movement in one direction for profits, and a breakout on the intraday chart can be the beginning of a move in that direction for the remainder of the day.

Chart courtesy of TrendSpider.com

The flat top pattern is a long and narrow trading range pattern like the $GLD chart. Price action stayed in a consolidation range from approximately $165 to $157 for roughly two months. This was the trading range, and the flat top resistance was in the $165 price zone. This was tested many times without breaking, keeping the resistance at the top flat. As price finally closed above $165, the chart became a flat top breakout.

The range in this pattern can be rectangular shaped or have irregular support levels. Both formations are valid if the top of the pattern at resistance is flat. The buy signal is on the breakout, and profit targets can be set at round numbers, an overbought reading or a trailing stop can be used to maximize profits.

This pattern can have a long price range consolidation period and needs a minimum of three tests of the resistance area to be called a flat top pattern. When price finally moves above the resistance and stays there, whether intraday or with a gap up at the open, this is a signal for the flat top breakout.

The trigger of the price breakout can be news, an earnings announcement or a business catalyst that finally pushes the buyers to overcome the sellers and make new highs over the old resistance. The breakout can continue to run in one direction as there is no pressure from trailing stops being triggered by holders, only profit targets signaling those traders should exit.

The flat top breakout pattern signal is more valid and has the potential for a bigger trend to emerge the longer the previous consolidation and longer the time frame. The pattern shows the path of least resistance for the future trend after the breakout occurs.

A breakout over resistance can signal a new uptrend in price.

36 STEVE BURNS & HOLLY BURNS

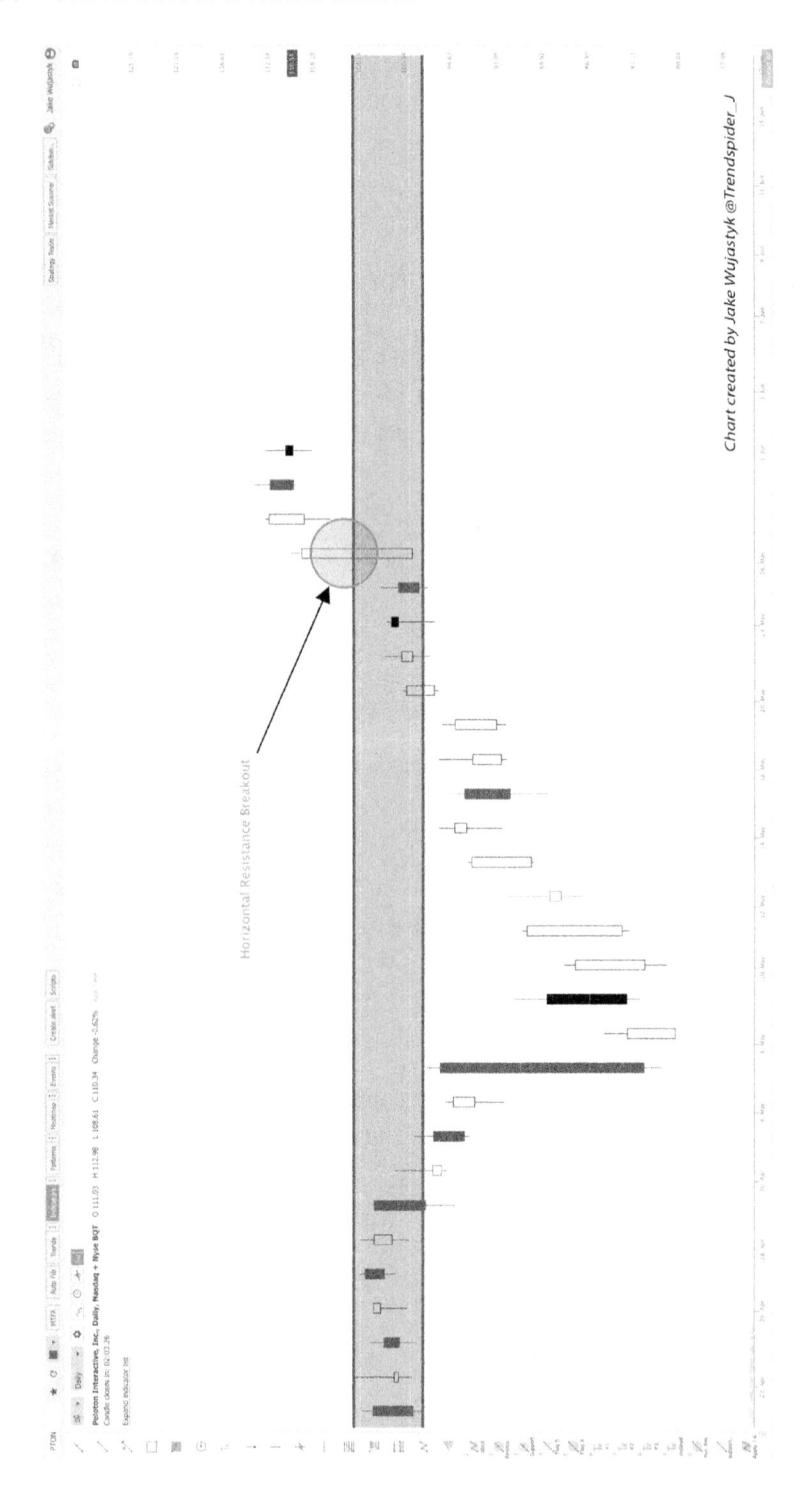

Chart created by Jake Wujastyk @Trendspider_J

A breakdown below support can signal a new downtrend in price.

38 STEVE BURNS & HOLLY BURNS

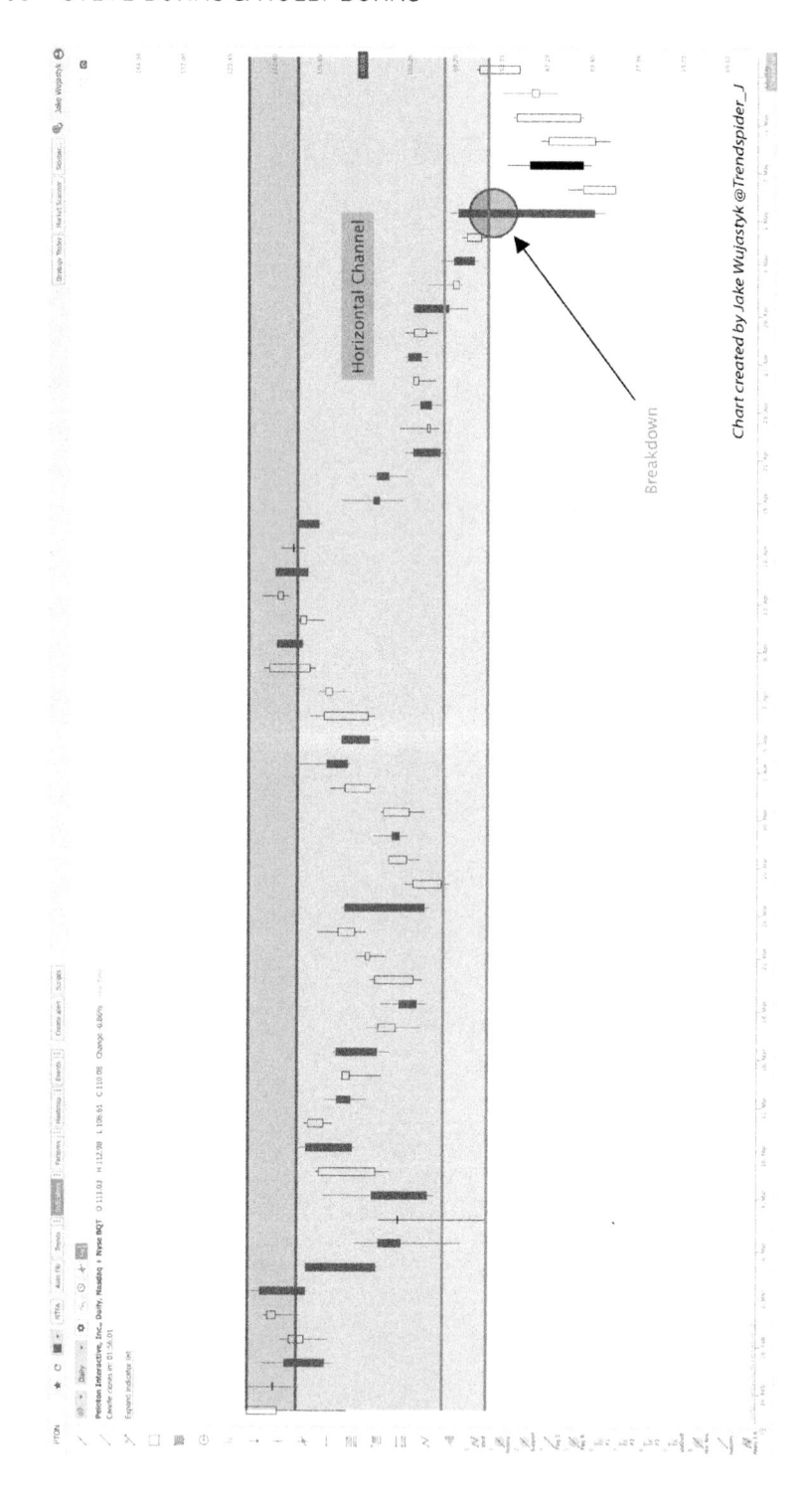

9

FIBONACCI LEVELS

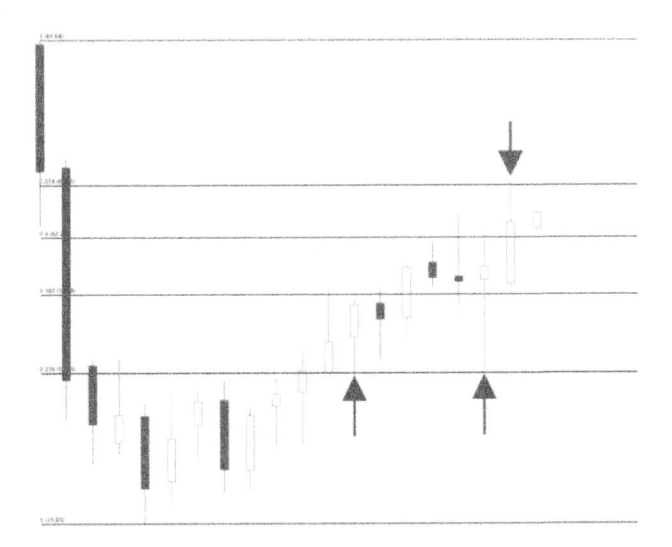

Fibonacci retracement is a trading methodology for determining high probability support and resistance levels on a chart. Its name comes from the use of the Fibonacci sequence. A Fibonacci retracement uses the theory that price swings on charts will usually retrace and backfill a mathematical portion of a move. After this measured pullback, the trend usually continues the move in the original direction.

A probable Fibonacci retracement level is quantified by taking two distant price points on a chart and dividing the vertical distance by using the key Fibonacci ratios. 0% is the starting point for the measurement of the retracement, and 100% is a complete reversal back to the starting point. Fibonacci levels are identified by measuring moves from the starting point of support or resistance. Horizontal trendlines are drawn on the chart to identify the potential key support and resistance levels. The significant levels of support or resistance to look for are 61.8% 50%, 38.2% and 23.6%.

A Fibonacci retracement is a common technical tool that price action traders use to look for high probability price levels for entries, to set stop losses in current trades or set profit targets on winning trades.

The concept of looking at key retracement levels at possible price extensions is a method not only used with Fibonacci, but also with many other methods like Elliott Wave theory. After an up or down swing in price, the new price support and resistance levels can be seen showing up at the key retracement levels in these methods.

While moving averages can change as price moves, the Fibonacci retracement levels are set prices and these targets on the chart always stay the same. This simplifies the identification of signals and creates price levels that can be acted on immediately. These levels are key reaction points on a chart and can lead to a binary action for traders as there is either a breakout in price or it is rejected and holds as support or resistance.

The primary 0.618 Fibonacci retracement price level used by so many stock traders is approximately the 'golden ratio'.

THE ULTIMATE GUIDE TO TECHNICAL ANALYSIS 41

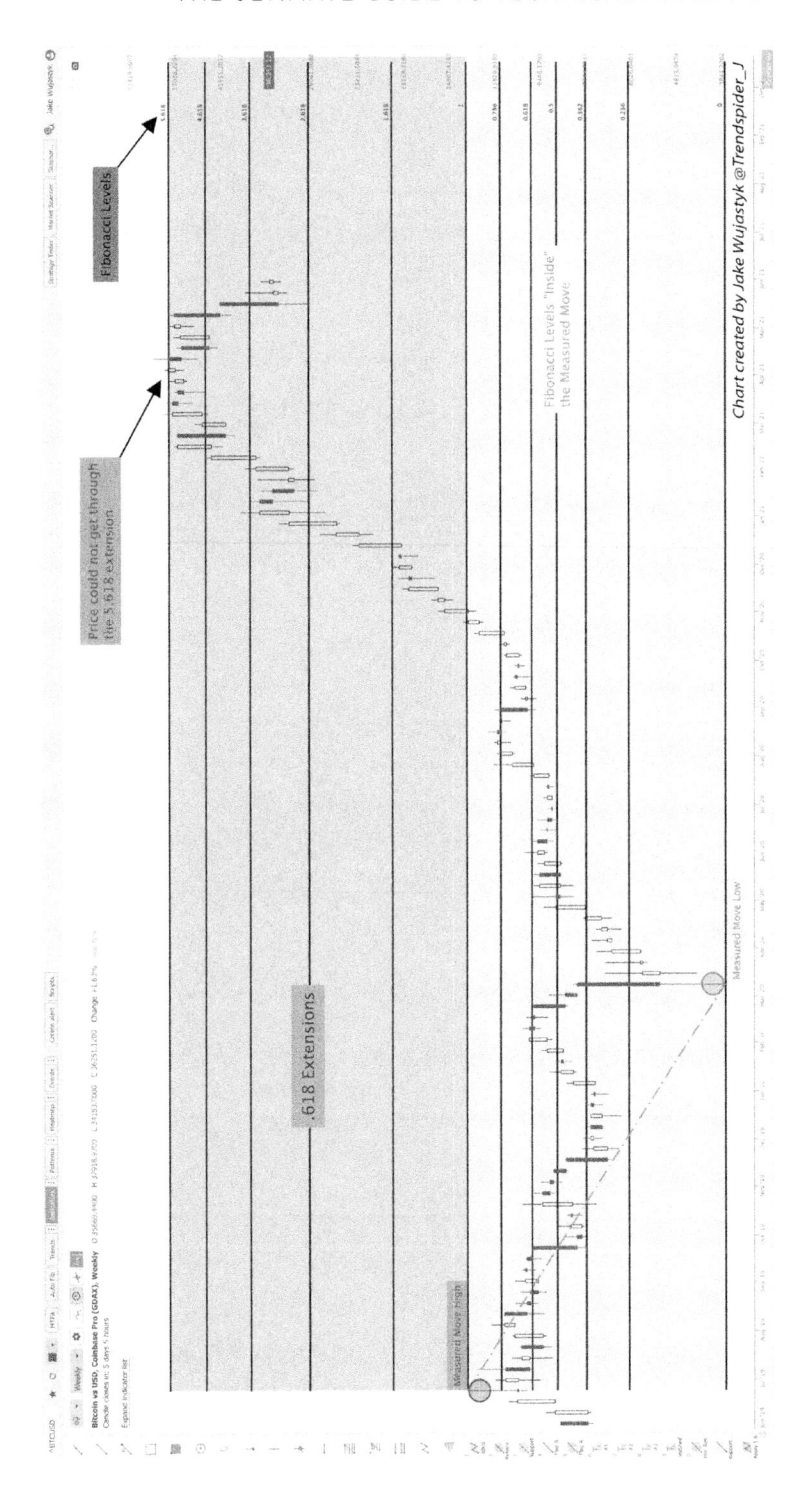

10

CHART PATTERNS

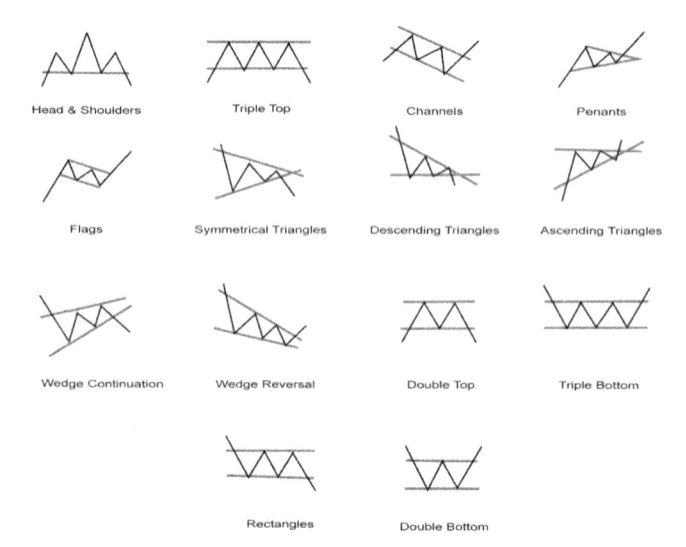

Head & Shoulders	Triple Top	Channels	Penants
Flags	Symmetrical Triangles	Descending Triangles	Ascending Triangles
Wedge Continuation	Wedge Reversal	Double Top	Triple Bottom
	Rectangles	Double Bottom	

Learning to read stock charts is one of the first skills a new trader should develop as their technical trading method, system and plan will emerge from this foundational skill. Reading stock charts will show the trader whether a chart is in an uptrend, downtrend, in a range or highly volatile.

Chart patterns are visual representations of the behaviors of buyers and sellers around different price levels. The importance of these levels emerges when they function as support or resistance. Chart patterns are bullish when a chart is making higher highs and higher lows, they're bearish when they make lower highs and lower lows, and range-bound when they have defined support and resistance levels and no trend.

Trading chart patterns is essentially momentum trading where a breakout of an existing pattern is the signal to enter a trade. Technical traders use the breakout of an existing trendline in a pattern to establish an entry point. After they are in the trade, it's managed to maximize a gain or minimize a loss to create a good risk/reward ratio. Chart patterns can signal breakouts, reversals and continuations of current price action.

A trendline on a chart can be drawn to show horizontal support or resistance in a range or vertical support or resistance in an uptrend. A chart pattern emerges to show the technical buying and selling price action of traders on the chart of a stock, commodity, currency or cryptocurrency.

How to read stock charts:

- Identify a pattern on a chart based on the parameters of price action.
- The more times a price support level or resistance level holds the more meaning it has.
- The longer a price range develops on a chart the greater the breakout and trend could be.
- Volume is like votes for a price at different levels. The greater the volume on a breakout, the higher the chance it will work out in the direction of the momentum. The highest peak volume also occurs many times near chart tops and bottoms before a reversal.

- In a bullish chart pattern, a buy signal is triggered on a break and follow through above a trendline of resistance of the existing price range consolidation after an upswing in price action. In a bearish chart pattern, a sell short signal is triggered on a break and follow through below a trendline of support of the existing price range consolidation after a downswing in price action.
- After a trade entry, a price target can be established based on previous resistance on a long-term chart, overbought readings for a bullish chart, previous support on a long-term chart or oversold readings for a bearish chart.
- A stop loss can be set at a reversal back through previous range support for a bullish pattern or a break back over previous range resistance for a bearish pattern.
- Position size should be conservative and not risk a big loss if the chart pattern doesn't follow through with a trend. 10% of total trading capital is a good position sizing parameter for most stock trades, less if a chart is volatile and more if an index ETF is being traded. For options and futures trading, it's a good idea to not risk more in position sizing than you are willing to lose, capping risk at 1% to 2% of total trading capital.
- Chart patterns can increase the odds of success by going with the trend and flow of current price action.

Chart patterns are not predictive tools, but they do show the direction a chart is likely to continue to go. When the momentum plays out and continues after a breakout, the magnitude of the profits can be many times greater than the loss that is minimized by a stop if the momentum ends. Chart patterns are ways to create good risk/reward ratios through reactive technical analysis.

Profitability usually comes from big wins and small losses, not from accuracy with a high win rate. Stock chart patterns can have big moves when the underlying company has the potential for huge growth in sales, revenue and profits.

Long-term stock trends can create more complex, classic chart patterns that play out through a full cycle of accumulation, distribution, and trading price action inside ranges.

Chart patterns are the visual clues that buyers and sellers leave at different price levels as they fight for control of the trend in a market.

Cup with handle bullish chart pattern example.

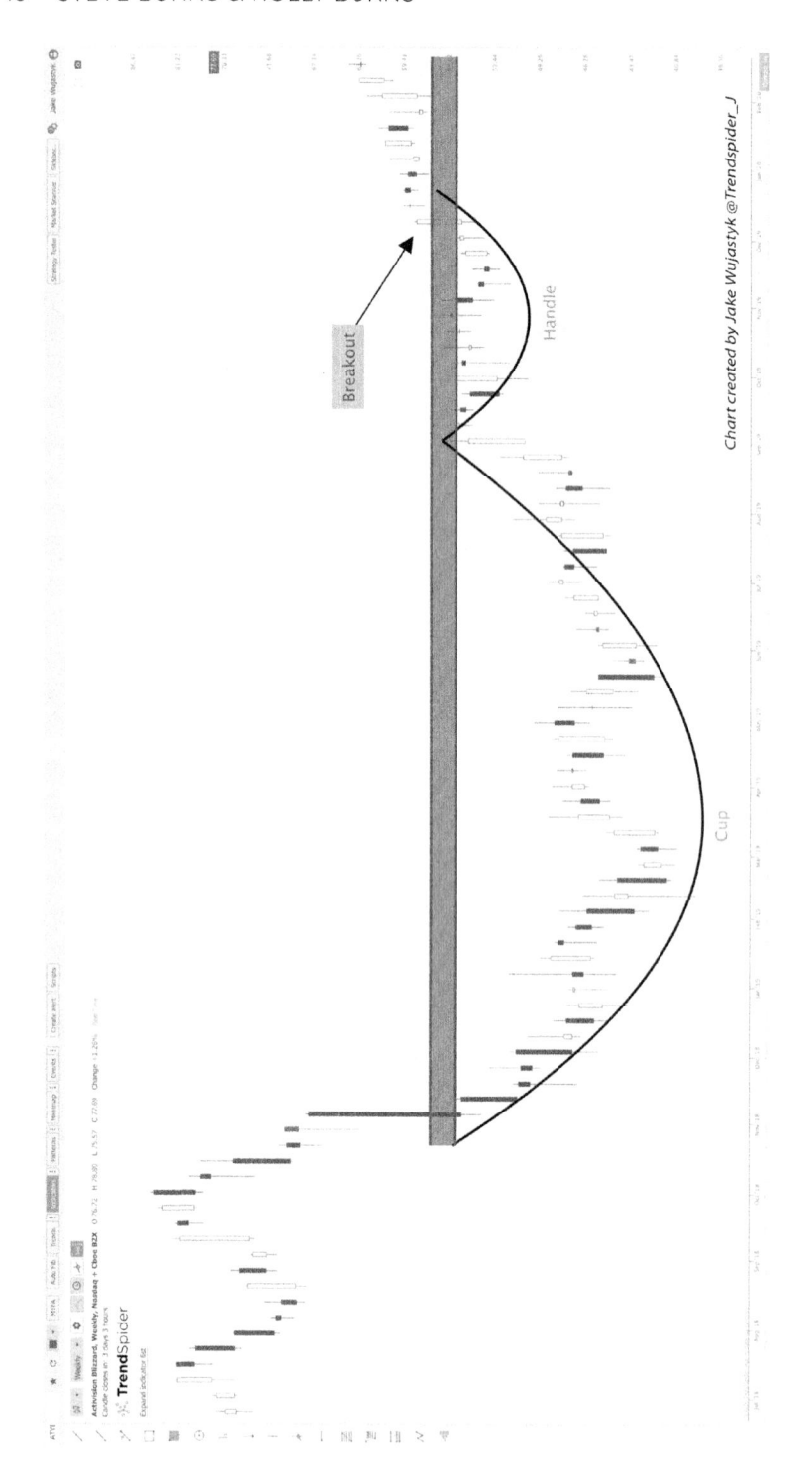

11

CANDLESTICK CHARTS

Colored Candlestick Combinations

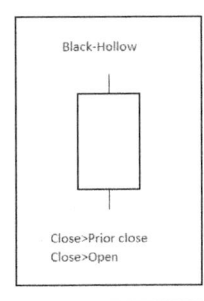

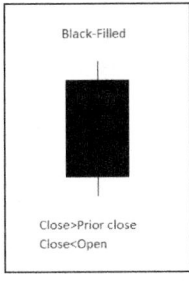

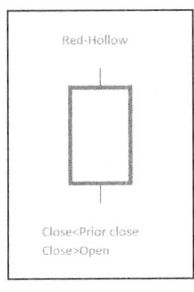

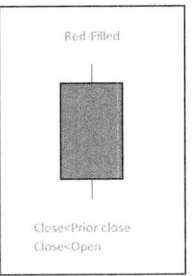

Black-Hollow

Close>Prior close
Close>Open

Red-Hollow

Close<Prior close
Close>Open

Black-Filled

Close>Prior close
Close<Open

Red-Filled

Close<Prior close
Close<Open

A candlestick is a type of chart used in trading as a visual representation of past and current price action in specified time frames.

A candlestick consists of the *body* with an upper or lower *wick* or *shadow*.

Most candlestick charts show a higher close than the open as represented by either a green or white candle, with the opening price near the bottom of the candle and the closing price near the top of the candle. Also, most candlestick charts show a lower close than the open represented by either a red or black candle, with the opening price close to the top of the candle body and the closing price near the low of the candle body.

Price action that happens outside the opening and closing prices of the period are represented by the wicks or shadows above the body of each candle. Upper wicks represent price action that occurred above the open, and the closing prices and the lower wicks represent price action that occurred below the opening and closing prices.

Candlesticks can be used in technical analysis to look for repeating patterns and in correlation with other technical indicators and signals.

Candlesticks are combined in many patterns to indicate the behavior of traders and investors when buying and selling in order to create good risk/reward setups for trading.

Candlestick charts have different settings. Candlesticks can be set to be green/red, or they can be set as hollow candles. With the green/red settings, the green candles occur when price closes higher than the previous close, and red candles occur if price closes lower than the previous close.

Colored Candlestick Combinations

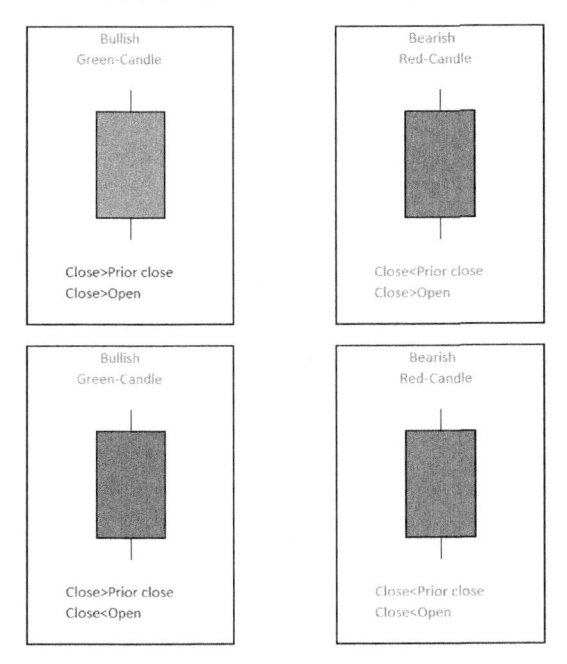

Bullish Green-Candle	Bearish Red-Candle
Close>Prior close / Close>Open	Close<Prior close / Close>Open
Bullish Green-Candle	Bearish Red-Candle
Close>Prior close / Close<Open	Close<Prior close / Close<Open

Hollow candlesticks are made up of four components in two groups. First, a close lower than the prior close gets a red candlestick and a higher close than the previous close gets a white candlestick. Second, a candlestick is hollow when the close is above the open and filled when the close is below the open. The following image shows the four possible hollow and filled candle combinations when using hollow candlestick chart settings.

Solid Red Candle

The solid red candle occurs when the candle closes below the previous candle's close and the close is lower than the open.

Hollow Grey Candle

The hollow grey candle occurs when the candle closes above the previous candle's close and the close is higher than the open.

The color of the candle is a function of the previous candle's close:
Higher close than previous candle = grey
Lower close than previous candle = red

The hollowness of the candle is a function of the candles close vs. open, nothing to do with the previous candle:
Hollow candle = close is higher than open
Solid candle = close is lower than open

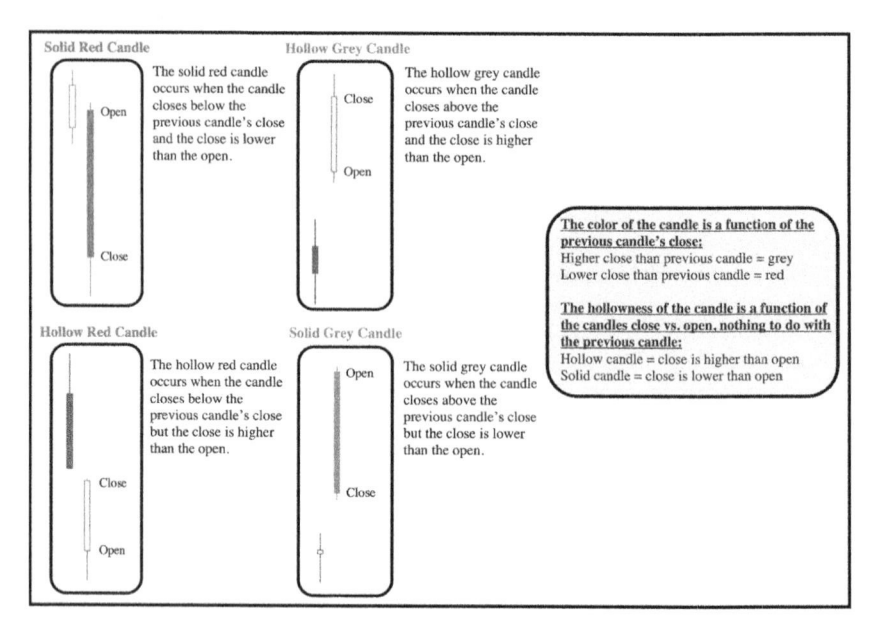

Hollow Red Candle

The hollow red candle occurs when the candle closes below the previous candle's close but the close is higher than the open.

Solid Grey Candle

The solid grey candle occurs when the candle closes above the previous candle's close but the close is lower than the open.

Image courtesy of Jake Wujastyk of TrendSpider.com

Red-hollow candlesticks can show some bullish reversal price action on an overall bearish chart. Even as the closing price was lower than the previous close, making the candle red, the price action moved higher during the period after the open making it hollow. Even though it closed lower than the previous trading period, there was buying pressure near the lows that made it close higher than the open.

The solid black or grey-candle is the inverse price action of the red-hollow candle. Although the closing price was above the previous close, making it black, price action finished lower than the open to make it a black-filled candle. Even though a black-filled candle closes higher on the current period versus the previous period, it does show selling pressure after the opening price. This candle illustrates rejection of intraday highs and can be a standalone signal of a bearish reversal during an upswing or uptrend in price action, especially near new highs in price.

There are four types of hollow candlesticks:

- Hollow candles occur when the price closed higher than it opened.
- Filled candles occur when the price closed lower than it opened.
- White candles occur when the price closed higher than the prior close.
- Red candles occur when the price closed lower than the prior close.

Note that white candles have black or grey outlines and may be called hollow black candles or hollow grey candles.

Learning to read candlesticks quickly is like learning a technical trading language. With time and experience, a trader can see what candles are indicating about the current price action. A trader can start seeing the patterns that emerge from buyers and sellers shifting the price action around key technical price levels of resistance and support. Multiple candlesticks in a row can show bullish, bearish or neutral chart patterns, so it's important to evaluate these signals in the context of the bigger picture on the chart.

Bearish candlestick patterns have better odds of success when they have confluence with other bearish signals, like overbought readings or a loss of key price support or an important moving average. The same applies with bullish candlestick patterns having better odds of success when they have confluence with other bullish signals, like oversold readings or breaking above a key price support or resistance area or retaking an important moving average.

Candlestick chart patterns illustrate the present and not the future. They can be used to increase the odds of capturing the next direction of price movement by aligning them in the path of least resistance. Profitable trading occurs by going with the current trend on a chart, letting winning trades run and cutting losing trades short with proper position sizing and discipline.

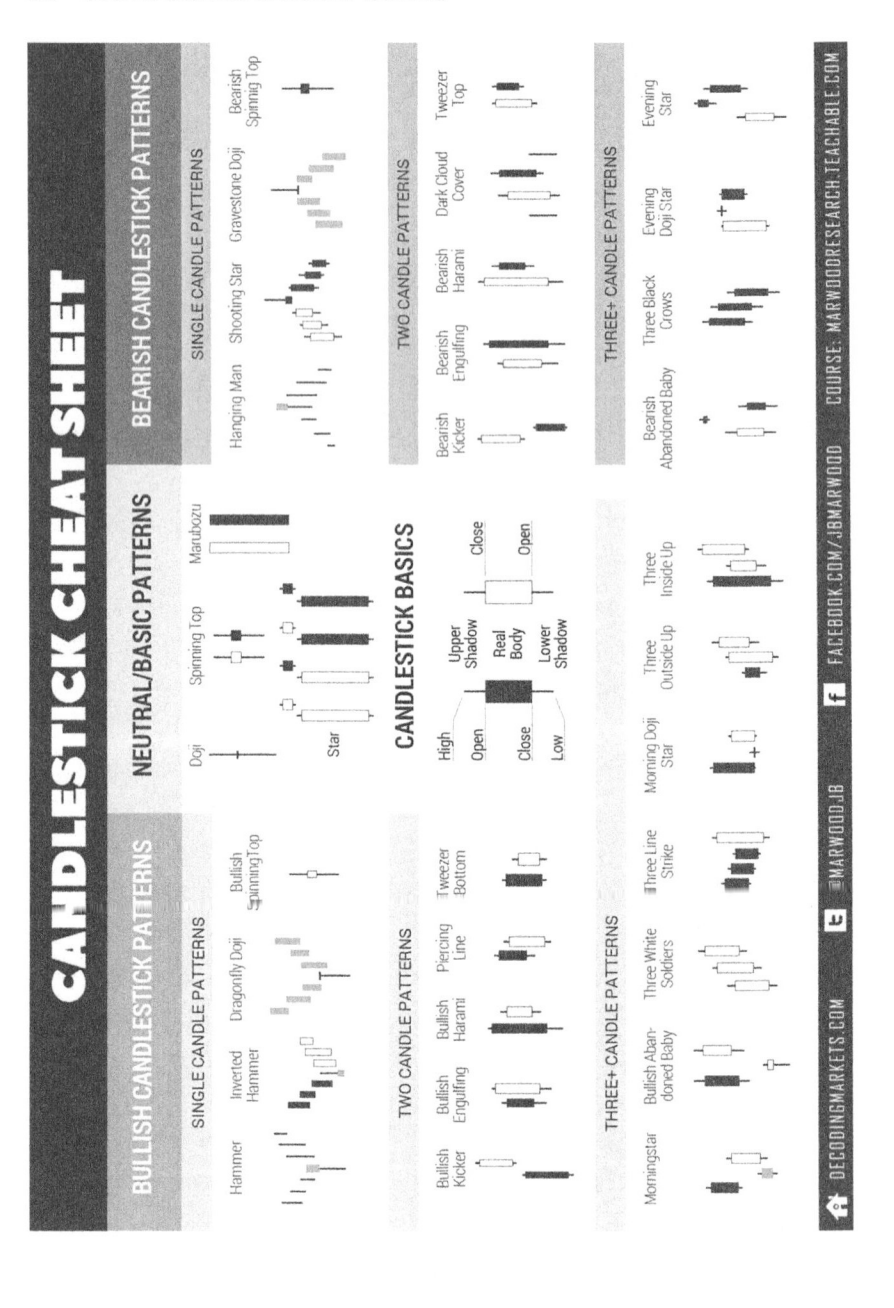

CANDLESTICK CHEAT SHEET

BULLISH CANDLESTICK PATTERNS

SINGLE CANDLE PATTERNS
- Hammer
- Inverted Hammer
- Dragonfly Doji
- Bullish Spinning Top

TWO CANDLE PATTERNS
- Bullish Kicker
- Bullish Engulfing
- Bullish Harami
- Piercing Line
- Tweezer Bottom

THREE+ CANDLE PATTERNS
- Morningstar
- Bullish Abandoned Baby
- Three White Soldiers
- Three Line Strike
- Morning Doji Star
- Three Outside Up
- Three Inside Up

NEUTRAL/BASIC PATTERNS
- Doji
- Spinning Top
- Marubozu
- Star

CANDLESTICK BASICS
- Upper Shadow
- Real Body
- Lower Shadow
- Open / Close
- High / Low

BEARISH CANDLESTICK PATTERNS

SINGLE CANDLE PATTERNS
- Hanging Man
- Shooting Star
- Gravestone Doji
- Bearish Spinning Top

TWO CANDLE PATTERNS
- Bearish Kicker
- Bearish Engulfing
- Bearish Harami
- Dark Cloud Cover
- Tweezer Top

THREE+ CANDLE PATTERNS
- Bearish Abandoned Baby
- Three Black Crows
- Evening Doji Star
- Evening Star

DECODINGMARKETS.COM @MARWOODJB FACEBOOK.COM/JBMARWOOD COURSE: MARWOODRESEARCH.TEACHABLE.COM

12

ELLIOTT WAVES

COMPLETE ELLIOTT WAVE

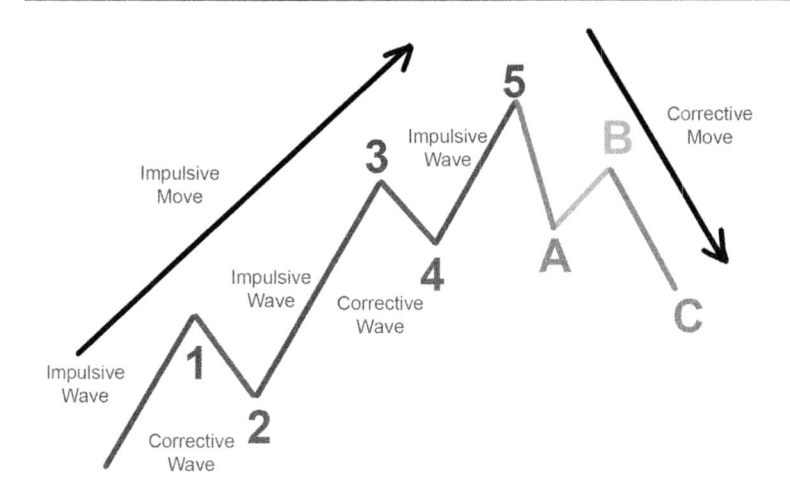

Elliott Wave Theory is a method of technical analysis that can be used to analyze and quantify price patterns in financial markets by looking at cycles. The theory proposes that changes in investor sentiment and their psychology creates impulse waves and corrective waves inside the larger trends in market price action.

The theory attempts to forecast market trends by identifying the extremes in trader's collective psychology that create the highs and lows in price action.

Ralph Nelson Elliott developed the theory of the underlying principles and created the analytical tools for trading it back in the 1930s. He believed that prices in markets play out in specific wave patterns, which his followers call *Elliott Waves*. In 1938, he published this theory of market behavior in his book, "The Wave Principle". He covered his principles more thoroughly in his final book, "Nature's Laws: The Secret of the Universe", published in 1946.

Elliott Wave analysts think that each wave has its own characteristic, which usually reflects the psychology of the current market move. Understanding these characteristics is thought to be the key to using these principles.

Elliott Wave definitions that follow apply during a bullish stock market; the characteristics are inverse during bear markets.

The five-wave pattern inside the dominant market trend.

ELLIOTT WAVE RULES

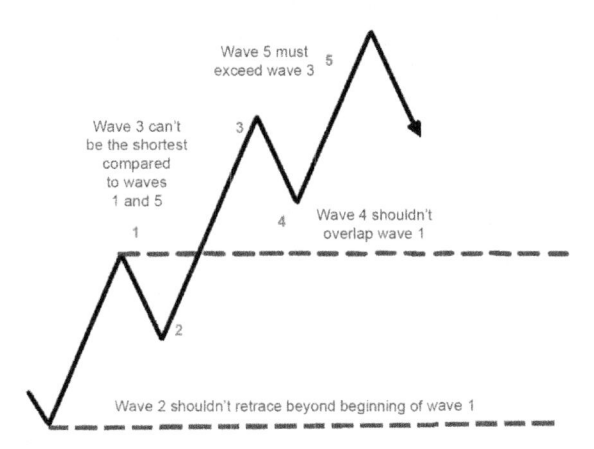

Figure: Elliott Wave diagram showing waves 1-5 with the following annotations:
- Wave 3 can't be the shortest compared to waves 1 and 5
- Wave 5 must exceed wave 3
- Wave 4 shouldn't overlap wave 1
- Wave 2 shouldn't retrace beyond beginning of wave 1

- **Wave 1:** Wave one is rarely obvious at inception. When the first wave of a new bull market begins, the fundamental news is typically negative. The previous trend is considered strongly in force, fundamental analysts continue to revise their earnings estimates lower and the economy doesn't look strong. Sentiment surveys are decidedly bearish, put options are popular and implied volatility in the options market is high. Volume might increase a small amount as prices rise, but not by enough to alert most technical traders.
- **Wave 2:** Wave two corrects wave one but can never extend beyond the starting point of wave one. Typically, the news is still bad. As prices retest the prior low, bearish sentiment quickly builds and the majority still insists that the bull market is still strong. Still, some positive signs appear for those who are paying attention. Volume should be lower in wave two than it was in wave one. Prices typically don't retrace more than 61.8% of the

wave one gains, and prices should fall in a three-wave pattern.

- **Wave 3:** Wave three is usually the largest and most powerful wave in a trend, although some research suggests that wave five is the largest in commodity markets. The news is now positive and fundamental analysts start to raise earnings estimates. Prices rise quickly, corrections happen briefly, and they are small. Anyone looking to get in on a pullback will likely miss the boat. As wave three starts, the news is probably still bearish, and most market players remain negative. However, by wave three's midpoint, *the crowd* will often join the new bullish trend. Wave three typically extends wave one by a ratio of 1.618:1.
- **Wave 4:** Wave four is typically corrective. Prices may meander sideways for an extended period, and wave four typically retraces 38.2% of wave three but it can be as much as 50% or 61.8%. Volume is well below that of wave three. This is a good place to buy a pullback if you understand the wave five potential. These waves are often frustrating because of their lack of progress in the larger trend.
- **Wave 5:** Wave five is the final leg in the direction of the dominant trend. The news is universally positive, and everyone is bullish. Unfortunately, this is when many average investors buy in, right before the top. Volume is often lower in wave five than in wave three, and many momentum indicators start to show bearish divergence; prices reach a new high, but the indicators don't reach a new peak. Looking back at 2000, 2007 and 2020, you can see how bears were dismissed when forecasting the top at the end of large bull markets.

The three-wave pattern corrective trend.

ELLIOTT WAVE FORMATION

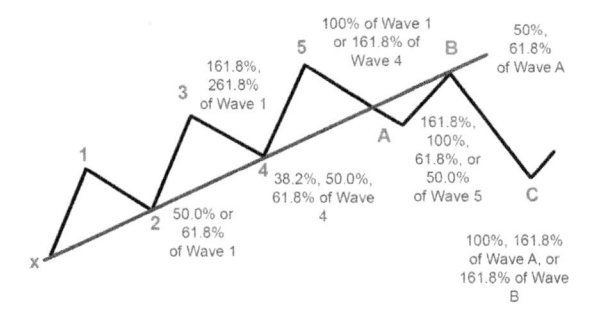

- **Wave A**: Corrections are typically harder to identify than impulse moves. In Wave A of a bear market, the fundamental news is usually still positive. Most analysts see the drop as a correction inside an active bull market. Some technical indicators that accompany Wave A include increased volume, rising implied volatility in the options markets and possibly a turn higher in open interest in related futures markets.
- **Wave B:** Prices reverse higher, which many see as a resumption of the now long-gone bull market. Those familiar with classical technical analysis may see the peak as the right shoulder of a head and shoulders reversal pattern. The volume during Wave B should be lower than in wave A. By this point, fundamentals probably aren't improving but they probably haven't turned negative.
- **Wave C:** Prices move impulsively lower in waves. Volume picks up, and by the third leg of Wave C, almost everyone realizes that a bear market is firmly in place.

Wave C is typically at least as large as Wave A and often extends to 1.618 times Wave A or beyond.

Elliott wave rules and guidelines:
A correct Elliott wave count must observe three rules:

- Wave two never retraces more than 100% of wave one.
- Wave three can't be the shortest of the three impulse waves, namely waves one, three and five.
- Wave four doesn't overlap with the price territory of wave one, except in the rare case of a diagonal triangle formation.

A common guideline called *alternation* observes that in a five-wave pattern, waves two and four often take alternate forms; a simple sharp move in wave two, for example, suggests a complex mild move in wave four. Corrective wave patterns unfold in forms known as zigzags, flats or triangles. These corrective patterns can come together to form more complex corrections. Similarly, a triangular corrective pattern is typically formed in wave four, but very rarely in wave two, and indicates the end of a correction.

Elliott Wave is a theory of price action designed to combine many principles of trading psychology, trend following and swing trading under one unifying theory of price action. The primary belief of Elliott was that market participants impulses of greed to buy creates the up waves and fear to sell create the corrections. Elliott wave traders attempt to profit from the moves by creating good risk/reward ratios in the path of least resistance as the waves play out.

THE ULTIMATE GUIDE TO TECHNICAL ANALYSIS   59

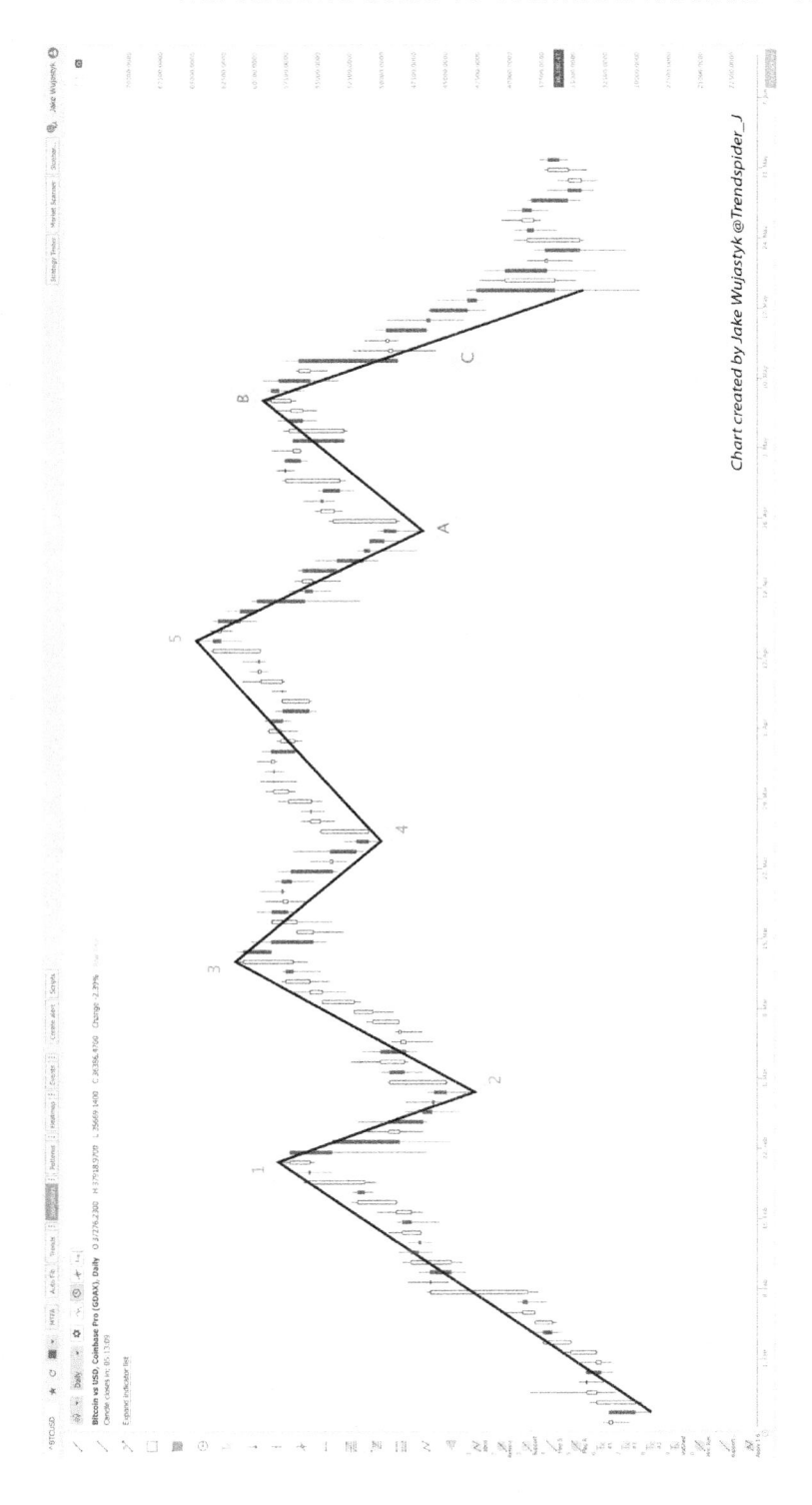

Chart created by Jake Wujastyk @Trendspider_J

13

TECHNICAL TREND INDICATORS

Moving Averages

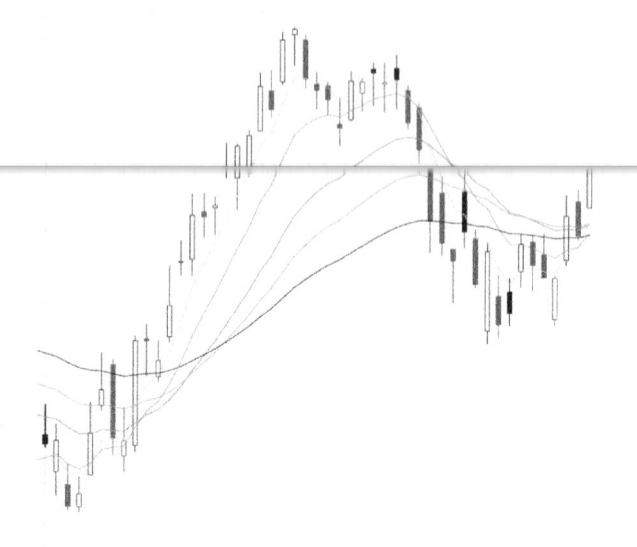

Moving average signals are trend following indicators that are designed to filter volatility and signal an entry and an exit on a chart to create large wins and small losses. Moving averages are quantified and can be backtested to see how they performed historically on price action charts.

Moving average signals are not predictive, they are reactive to a current price trend and their profitability comes from creating good risk/reward ratios. A moving average signal on a specific market can be validated through backtesting, and if it's shown to be profitable, it can be used as a management tool to capture trends and manage losing trades in the future.

Moving averages have been used as trading tools by many legendary traders and are a standard amongst many trend trading systems. They can be used on different time frames to capture trends. Moving averages can be used as entry signals on a trade, and as exit signals to quantify stop losses for a losing trade, or a trailing stop for winning trades.

Moving average signals are one part of a trading system, but it's still necessary to build a watchlist of stocks, ETFs, currencies or commodities that have the best odds of a future trend in price. A trader must also position size each trade based on their own risk management parameters.

The moving average signals used by swing traders and trend traders typically beat buy and hold in the backtested stock or ETF. When backtesting, be aware that even if a signal doesn't beat buy and hold, it could still beat the risk adjusted returns for buy and hold. To get the buy and hold returns a trader must take the same levels of constant risk that an investor takes. Going to cash with a moving average exit signal lowers your risk exposure over the long-term and can improve your risk adjusted returns because of less required holding time.

Moving average signals can keep you from losing money during downtrends and bear markets as they tell you to go to cash or sell short. They also look great when in an uptrend or upswing in price and making money. Volatility and whipsaw reversals in price action are the biggest disruptors of moving average signals because they create false signals. However, they generally keep a trader on the right side of a trend in the time frame of the moving averages used.

Moving averages can be better than investment advice because they identify the current trend and don't try to predict the future. Use moving average signals to create a quantified backtested trading system with an edge. Everyone must trade based on their own time frame, risk tolerance and return goals, so the moving averages that a trader uses will be determined by their own strategy.

Your watchlist is the first filter in a trading system. Moving average signals are designed to capture uptrends in price so it's important to have a watchlist of stocks, ETFs, currencies or commodities that tend to trend higher in price over time. A market and chart that have a history of consistently making new all-time highs are the best candidates.

Stock market index ETFs are a good place to start when building a watchlist because they are systematically designed to remove losing stocks and bring in new winning stocks, making new all-time highs over time. This means that you'll always have an opportunity to participate in trading a group of the biggest winning stocks, which is especially powerful when trend trading in bull markets.

Creating a watchlist of leading stocks also creates opportunities to use moving average signals to create gains during large uptrends in price. The best stocks are for companies with new products, good business models, innovative technologies and sometimes create new industries. Filtering for underlying company fundamentals can help create a winning watchlist of stocks. When analyzing stocks, it's important to look for sales growth, increasing revenue, rising profits and expanding market share.

Many of the best stocks will be near all-time highs in price or be close to 52-week high in price. Pressing near new price highs is one of the strongest technical indicators. However, that doesn't mean that you should buy them and chase them higher. Instead, put them on your watchlist and wait for a pullback and a new moving average signal.

Backtest stocks that fit your filter for quality in technical price action and quality fundamentals. What you decide to put on your watchlist, and trade should be limited to stocks you have already backtested and confirmed that the signals worked in the past. Your watchlist of stocks, ETFs, commodities and currencies should be those that pass your backtest filters and show good historical trends.

The moving average signals used to trade a watchlist should show profitability in the specific asset being researched. Different assets tend to have various levels of historical volatility and you must adjust accordingly. Some stocks are low volatility and work out better for buy and hold investors, while others swing and trend, giving moving averages a trading edge.

The best risk/reward ratio is usually created by entering a moving average signal at the time it's triggered. You may experience diminished rewards if it started trending higher days or weeks ago. It's typically better to wait for a pullback and new set up than to chase a trend already underway.

One thing that is difficult to quantify is the survivor bias in these backtests. When trading a watchlist of stocks, moving average cross-under exit signals can help filter out losing stocks and signal when to go to cash. This helps you sell underperforming stocks that lose their key moving average crossovers. You must consider not only the money you make staying long in the right stocks in uptrends, but also the money you save by not being long in the wrong stocks in down-trends. Stocks that become volatile or continue to make lower highs and lower lows should be removed from your watchlist until they begin performing better.

Another strength of moving average systems with a diversified watchlist is the ability to maximize returns through the rotation of capital to charts with the best trends. Moving average signals give you the ability to rotate out of stocks that are no longer trending upward and into others with favorable trend signals. Even if signal backtest returns don't look impressive on their own, it'll be just one allocation of capital inside your system. When the chart signal says go to cash, the capital could be creating gains in another trend on your watchlist.

A moving average is a technical indicator that you can use to quantify price trends and trading signals.

Moving averages can be used for the following:

- Entry signal- It can be a signal to buy when price crosses over a single moving average or two moving averages cross over each other.
- Exit signal- It can be a signal to sell when price crosses under a single moving average or two moving averages cross under. Price breaking back over a key moving average or a new moving average crossover can be a signal to buy to cover a short position.
- Trailing stop- A short-term moving average can be used as a trailing stop loss to allow a winning trade to run until it reverses and closes under that moving average.
- Stop loss- A loss can be limited when entering a long trade by using a moving average as the place to exit the trade if it fails to hold as support. When a short trade is entered, a loss can be limited by using a moving average as the place to exit the trade if it fails to hold as resistance.
- Profit target- A price move back to a key, higher moving average can be the target where profits are locked in.
- To scale into a position- A trade can be scaled into as key moving averages are retaken. For instance, after a downtrend, buy on a break back over the 250-day moving average and then add more to the position as the 200-day moving average is retaken.
- Trend indicator- Where price is in relation to the moving average in your time frame can tell you the direction of the current price trend in a market. Price

over the 50-day moving average could be a current uptrend signal, while price under the 200-day moving average may be the signal of a current downtrend in price.
- Risk management- Using moving averages as stop losses, trailing stops and trend signals can help you manage risk by limiting your losses in capital and open profits in a position.
- Quantify position sizing- You can size your trade based on your moving average stop loss level according to how much you want to lose if the trade doesn't go your way.
- Measure of volatility- How far price is from a moving average in a time frame can show the level of volatility and deviations the price currently is from the average price.
- Manage volatility- Moving average crossovers of two moving averages as entry and exit signals can filter out much of the noise in price action and focus on the larger trend.
- Creating good risk/reward ratios- Using moving averages to set a stop loss much smaller than your potential profit target gain can create good risk/reward ratios.
- Trade management- Moving averages can be used to cut losses short and let winners run by managing a trade as it evolves, moving from a stop loss to a trailing stop, and potentially a profit target.
- Quantifying signals for backtesting- Moving average signals can be quantified and used in backtesting to analyze their historical performance as mechanical entry and exit signals.

Moving averages are tools for identifying, quantifying and trading trends on a chart in the time frame of your choice. They can be used in correlation with other technical indicators to create the best risk/reward ratios from entry to exit in the path of least resistance.

Chart courtesy of TrendSpider.com

Moving Average Convergence Divergence (MACD)

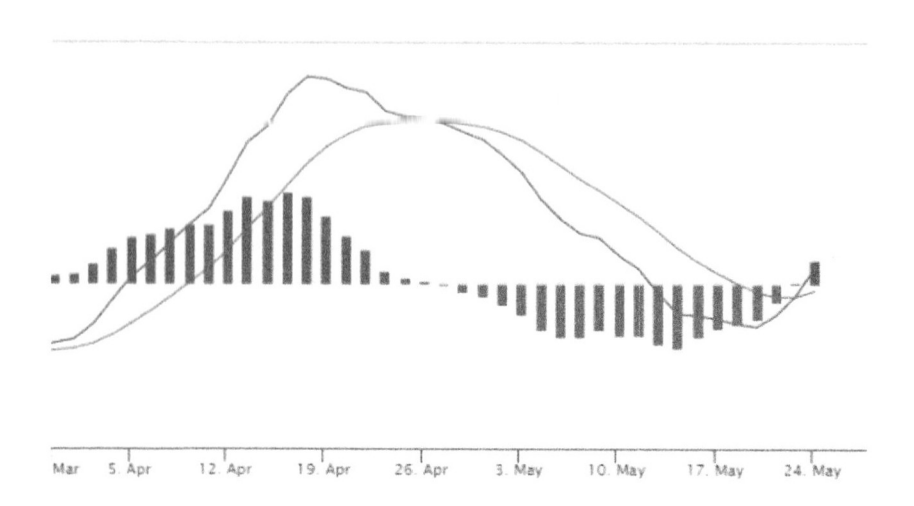

MACD (Mack-Dee) is the abbreviation for the moving average convergence/divergence technical indicator. The MACD is an indicator used in technical analysis to filter and trade the momentum of price action on a chart. It was created by Gerald Appel in the late 1970s as a tool for technical analysts, and was designed to indicate changes in price strength, direction, momentum and duration for trends and swings in price action on a chart.

The MACD is a simple visual momentum indicator. It takes two moving averages that act as trend following indicators and creates a momentum oscillator by subtracting the longer-term moving average from the shorter-term moving average. This formula creates the MACD as a double indicator for both trend identification and magnitude of momentum. The MACD lines fluctuate above and below the zero line on the histogram as the moving averages come together, crossover and separate.

How to use MACD

Traders can wait for signal line crossovers, center line crosses and divergences as potential trading signals. The MACD is not bound inside set parameters, so it's not a useful tool for identifying extended overbought or oversold price levels. It's a trend and momentum indicator that indicates the current direction of a move.

The MACD is calculated by subtracting the 26-period exponential moving average from the 12-period exponential moving average. The result of the calculation is the MACD line. The nine-day EMA of the MACD is called the signal line. This is the faster signal line that is with the MACD line, and it can function as a crossover trigger for buy and sell signals in the direction of the price move to capture trends or swings. Many traders use it as a buy signal when the chart shows the signal line crossing above its MACD line. They then lock in profits when the signal line crosses back below the MACD line. The MACD indicator can be used in many ways, but it is commonly used for crossovers and divergences to create signals.

The bar chart in the background of the MACD histogram quantifies the difference between the MACD line and the signal line. When the MACD line is above the signal line, the bar is positive.

When the MACD is below the signal line, the bar is negative. The size of the bar is the difference between the MACD line and signal line for each period on the chart. This is a clear visual representation of the magnitude of a move in one direction based on the correlation of the MACD lines.

The bullish signal line MACD crossover can show momentum and a possible swing higher in price that can evolve into a sustained trend. A bullish crossover can happen near a price bottom after a rally off the lows, or when price emerges out of a price range. A bearish MACD signal line cross under can show the loss of momentum early when a trend turns into a trading range and fails to make new highs. A bearish MACD cross under can also signal the beginning of a downtrend and the end of an uptrend.

The MACD works best when used with other technical indicators for confirmation. For example, if you use MACD crosses to get into a trade you could use the Relative Strength Index (RSI) to exit and lock in gains as a chart becomes overbought in the 70 RSI zone or oversold in the 30 RSI zone. Also, if you have a key moving average crossover signal on a chart, a bullish MACD cross can confirm the trade with a confluence and give the trade greater odds of success.

The MACD can help trade price action on a chart by showing the current directional bias along with key turning points. MACD shows the current momentum of price action and the path of least resistance.

THE ULTIMATE GUIDE TO TECHNICAL ANALYSIS   69

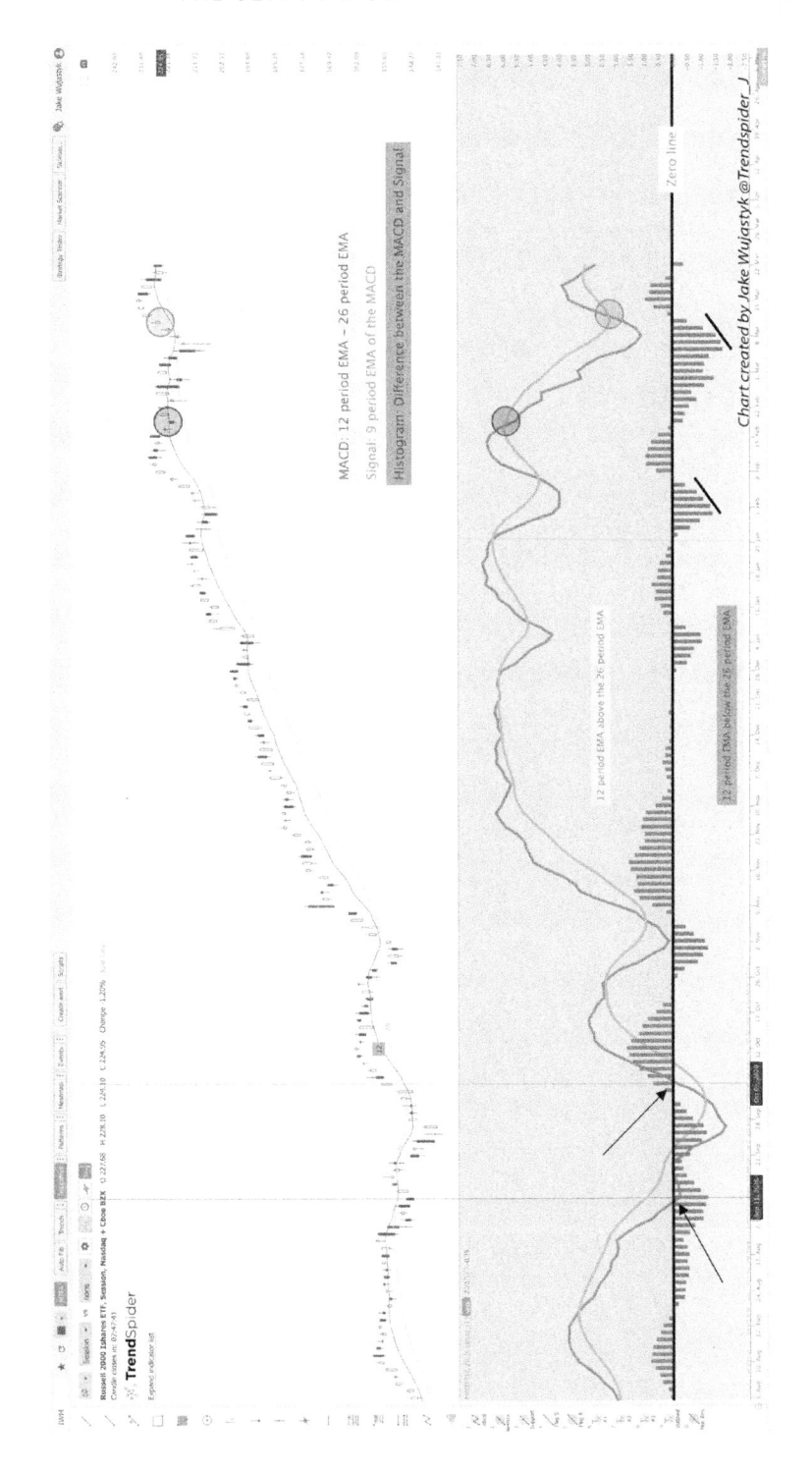

14

TECHNICAL MOMENTUM INDICATORS

Stochastic Oscillator

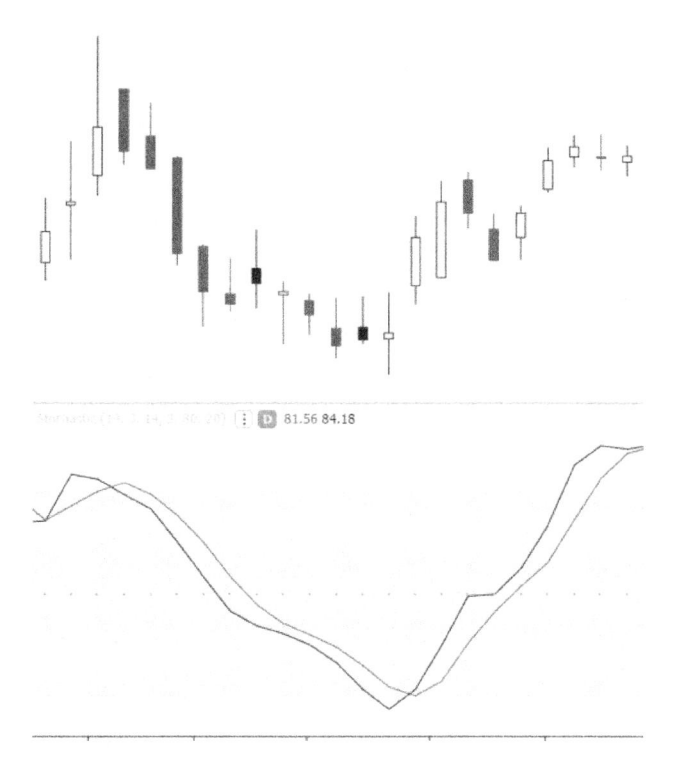

The Stochastic Oscillator is a momentum indicator that measures the location of the closing price on a chart in relation to the high to low trading range over a period. This indicator was created by George C. Lane in the late 1950s. The Stochastic Oscillator doesn't follow the trend in price or volume, instead it quantifies the speed and momentum of price action on a chart.

On most charts, the momentum of price movement changes before its directional move. Bullish or bearish divergences in the Stochastic Oscillator can signal with a high degree of confidence, that a reversal in price action is close. Divergences are the most common signal used with the Stochastic Oscillator.

The Stochastic Oscillator should always be moving in correlation with price action, and both should set highs or lows at the same time, depending on the direction of the trend. Bearish divergences are signaled when a new high in price happens, but the Stochastic Oscillator doesn't set a new high at the same time. Bullish divergences are signaled when price makes a new lower low with the Stochastic Oscillator forming a higher low. This loss of correlation may show that either trend could be losing momentum in its current direction and be near reversing in the opposite direction. After a divergence is signaled, a trader should look for a confluence of other indicators to confirm the reversal, like candlestick reversal patterns or rejections near key moving averages.

When the Stochastic Oscillator breaks above the 50-center line it's considered bullish for upside momentum. A break below the 50-center line can be bearish, indicating downside momentum in price action.

The Stochastic Oscillator is a range-bound technical indicator and can be used for quantifying overbought and oversold levels in price action after a trend goes too far and too fast in one direction with no pullback. This oscillator has a reading range from a low of zero to a maximum of one hundred. Regardless of the speed, as price moves higher or lower, the Stochastic Oscillator will stay in this set range.

The most common use of the Stochastic Oscillator is to read 80 as overbought and 20 as oversold on a chart. These levels can be set based on the needs of a specific chart looking at historical behavior. A reading over 80 for the 20-day period of the Stochastic Oscillator shows that the stock is trading near the top of its own 20-day high-low range. A reading below 20 shows that a stock is trading at the low level of its 20-day high-low range.

The Stochastic Oscillator is above 50 when the closing price is in the upper half of the trading range, and it's below 50 when the closing price is in the lower half of the trading range. A low reading of below 20 signals that price may be near the low on the chart for the period. A high reading of above 80 signals that price may be near the high for the period. Charts tend to stay within the 20/80 readings during range-bound markets but break above or below during strong trends.

There is both a fast and slow Stochastic Oscillator, and either can be used based on a trader's need for the speed of entries and exits based on their chosen time frame. The Stochastic Oscillator verifies a trader is on the right side of price action based on the speed and momentum of the path of least resistance.

74 STEVE BURNS & HOLLY BURNS

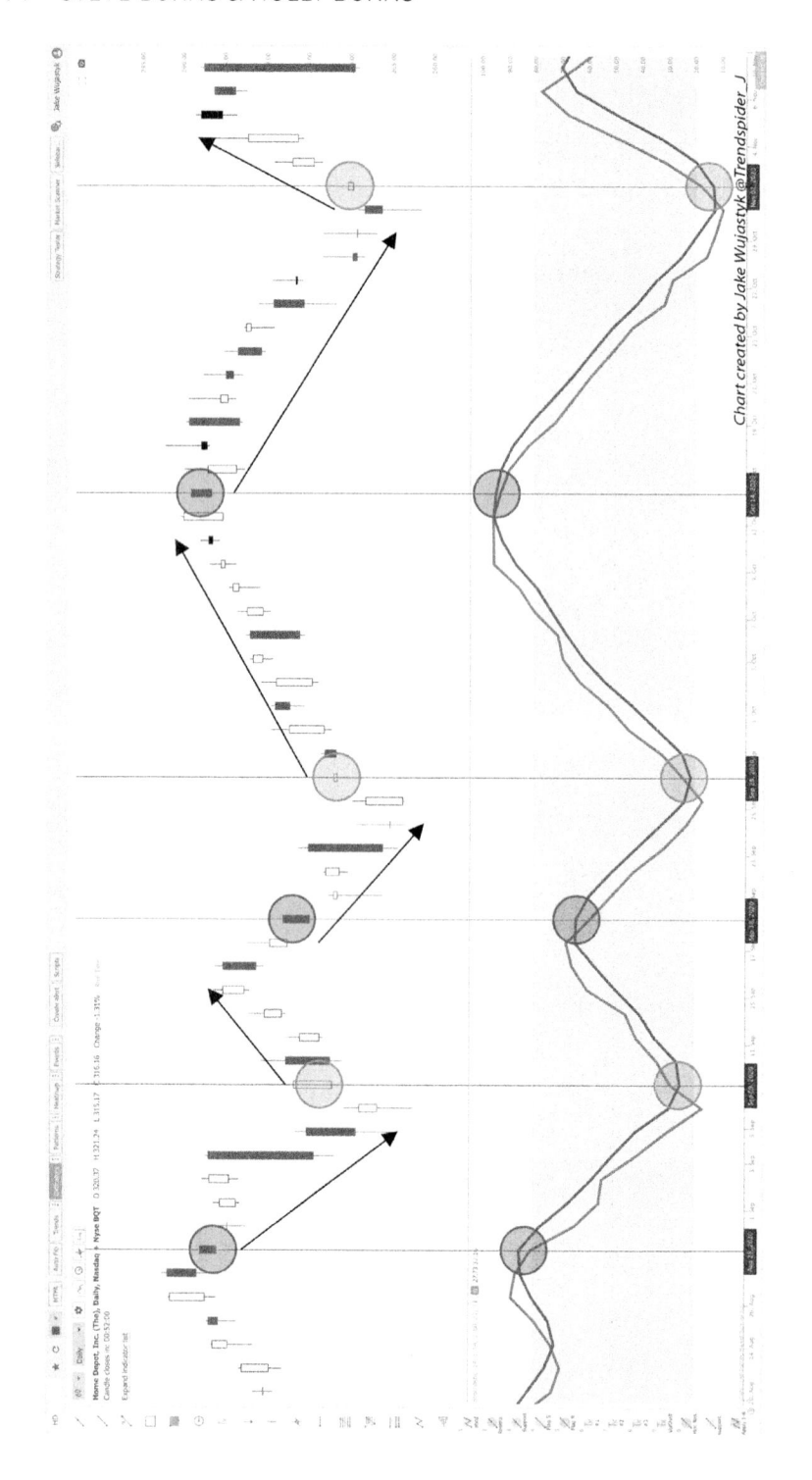

Commodity Channel Index (CCI)

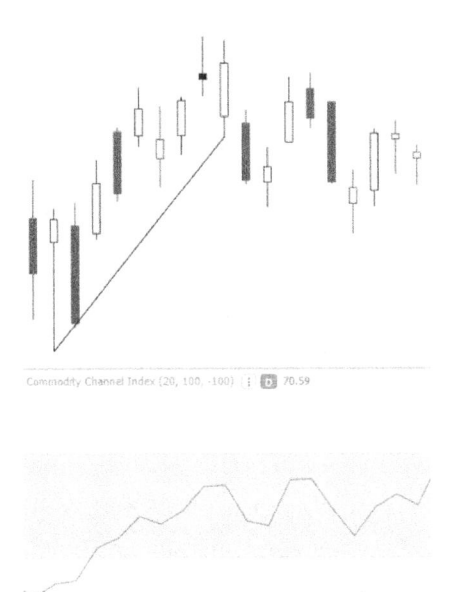

The CCI indicator (commodity channel index) is an oscillator originally created in 1980 by Donald Lambert. He developed CCI to identify and quantify cyclical moves in commodity charts, but this technical indicator has also been used on stocks, stock indexes, exchange traded funds, and charts of other markets.

It can be used as a diverse indicator to signal a price trend on a chart, or as a warning sign of overbought or oversold conditions. It can signal the beginning of a new trend on a chart or that a current trend has gone too far and too fast, indicating that it could reverse soon.

The CCI indicator measures the current price in relation to the average price over a specified time frame. CCI has a high reading when prices are above their average and has a low reading when current prices are below their average for the time frame. CCI can be used to quantify overbought and oversold areas through the level of its current reading on a chart.

The number of CCI periods set on a chart is used to calculate the simple moving average and mean deviation. Lambert set the constant at .015, so 70% to 80% of CCI values would be in the -100 to +100 range. Where a sample percentage of the CCI indicator reading falls within its ranges is determined on the period examined. A shorter period has more volatility and a smaller percentage of values in the +100 to -100 range. A longer period has a higher percentage of +100 to -100 reading values.

High positive CCI readings can signal that price levels are far above their average price at a specific time, showing price strength. A low negative CCI reading can signal that price levels are far below their average price and indicates price weakness.

The CCI indicator can be used as a trend indicator. When the CCI moves above +100 it signals momentum and potential uptrending price action. When the CCI indicator moves below -100, it signals falling price momentum and potential downward price action.

Technical analysts can use the CCI indicator as a leading indicator for a reversal by analyzing if extreme overbought or oversold readings are signaling a high probability of a mean reversion in price back near the 0-line. Bullish and bearish divergences are used to observe slowing momentum and the potential for trend reversals. When price makes a new high, but CCI doesn't make a new high reading, it's considered a bearish divergence. When price makes a new low, but CCI doesn't make a new low reading, it's considered a bullish divergence.

The CCI indicator gives a trader context to the momentum and duration of a price move in relation to the average price in a chart's time frame, showing not only momentum of the trend, but also acting as a signal.

THE ULTIMATE GUIDE TO TECHNICAL ANALYSIS 77

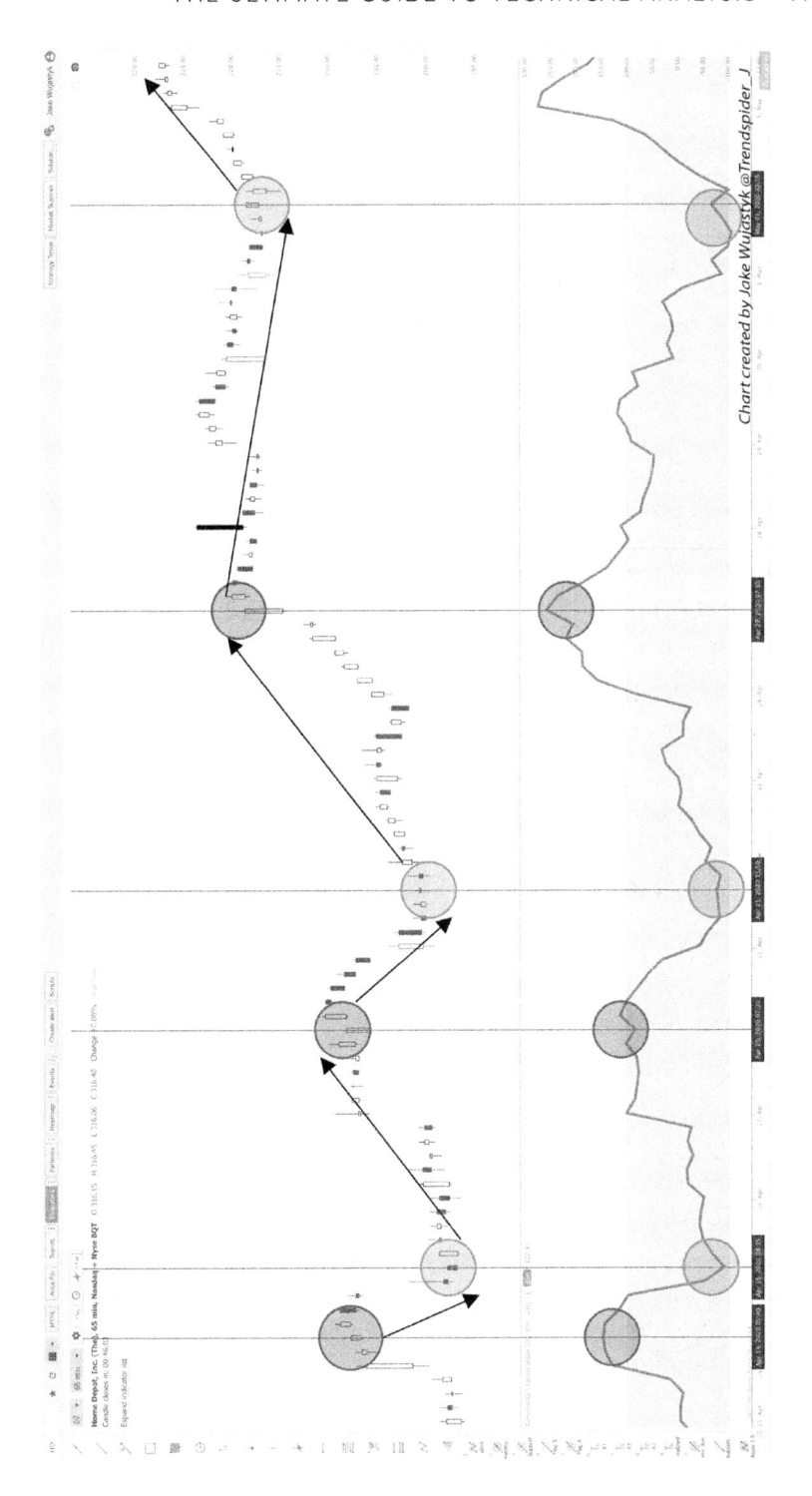

Relative Strength Index (RSI)

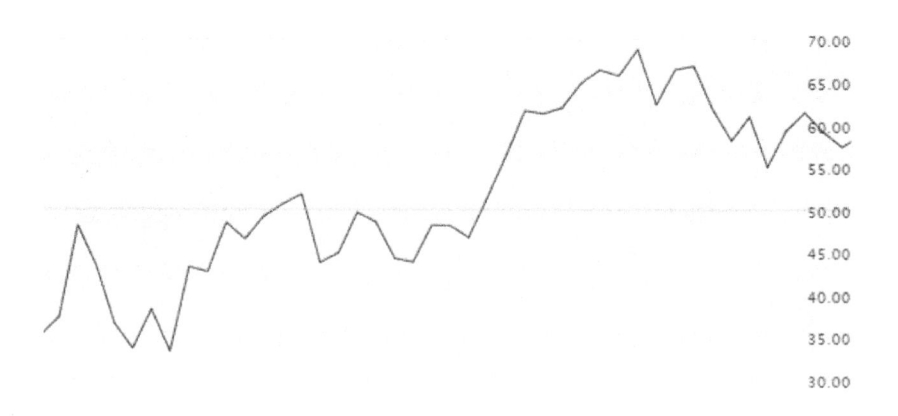

The RSI (Relative Strength Indicator) is a momentum oscillator that measures the speed and change in price movements. The RSI moves in a bounded range between 0 and 100. The default setting on a chart for RSI is 14. The RSI is generally overbought when its reading is above 70 and oversold when it reads below 30. Signals can also be generated by looking for divergences between RSI and price action as one makes a higher high or lower low and the other doesn't. Parabolic breakouts below 30 or above 70 on a closing basis and centerline crossovers of the 50 reading can be signals of momentum. RSI can also be used to identify the current trend of the market, because price is generally above the 50 RSI in an uptrend and below the 50 RSI during a downtrend.

The RSI can be used as a dip buy entry signal looking to buy the strongest stocks or index ETFs when price is near the 30 RSI reading. Bounces at the 30 RSI can confirm support or a break below and back above the 30 RSI to confirm it's near a bottom, and that oversold price levels have been rejected by sellers. The 50 RSI level is usually a good reward target on a 30 RSI entry.

When long during uptrends, a trader can look to exit and lock in profits when the 70 RSI is reached and starts to become resistance. If price breaks above and closes higher than the 70 RSI, continuing to hold a long position has the potential of catching a big win when a parabolic uptrend continues to move higher.

Personally, I consider the RSI indicator as an oscillator that measures risk/reward ratio. As it nears 30, the reward favors the buyer, because a stock or index has moved too far down and too fast, indicating that it may bounce. At the 70 RSI, the reward for long positions starts to diminish in most cases, as a stock or index becomes overbought after having gone up too far and too fast. It's more probable that a stock can move from a 50 RSI to a 70 RSI than to move from a 70 RSI to a 90 RSI. It's not impossible, just less likely in most cases. Parabolic trends under the 30 RSI and over the 70 RSI are rare but can be large moves when they do happen.

A market will spend most of its time inside the 30/70 RSI boundaries and rarely leave this range. Combining the best stocks that are in demand with 30 RSI dips increases the odds of success, because there may be buyers looking to get in at the oversold area on the chart. Parabolic extended trends are what typically breaks the bounds of the RSI. The value zone is in the 50 RSI range and price tends to return to that area over time.

The RSI is not a perfect signal every time because nothing works all the time, as the market is always changing its price action dynamics. A trader must always use proper risk management with any signal, but it's a great tool for quantifying the oversold and overbought parameters for stocks on a watchlist for a higher probability set up and trade management.

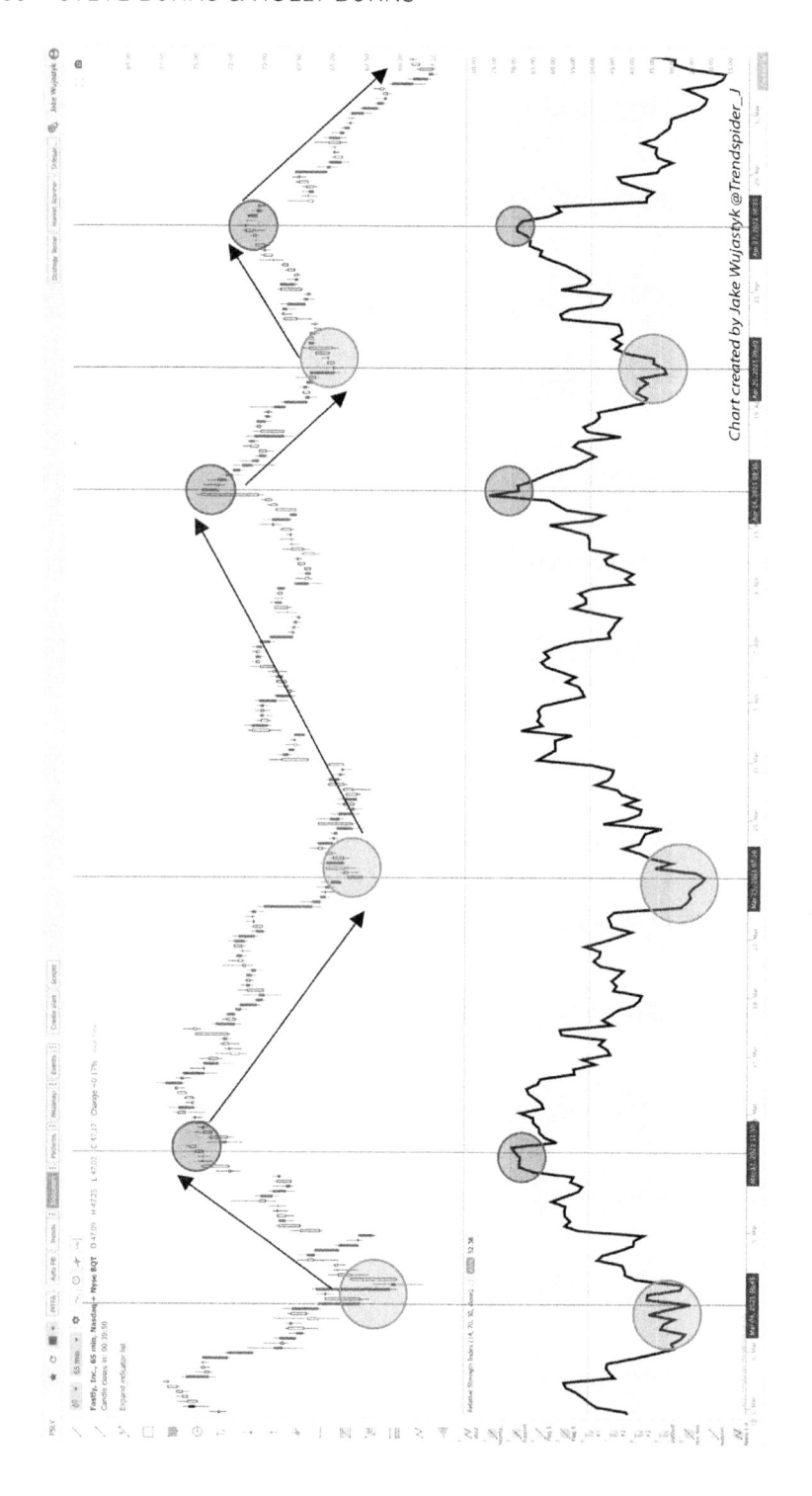

15

TECHNICAL VOLATILITY INDICATORS

Bollinger Bands®

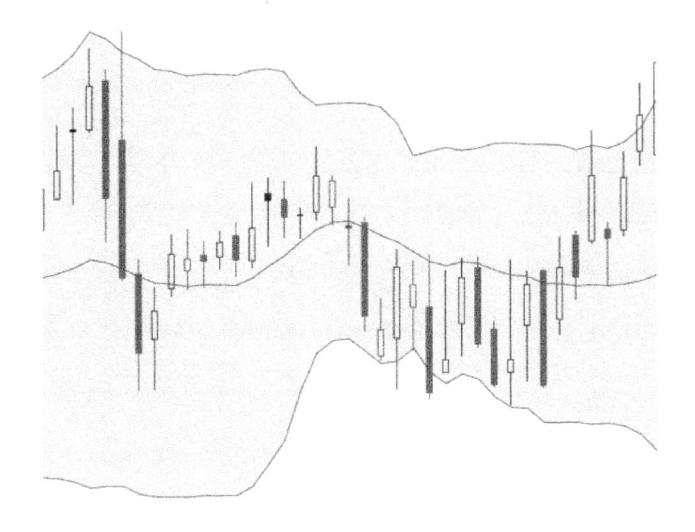

B ollinger Bands® are a technical indicator created by John Bollinger in the 1980s.* They were created to form a quantified visual trading range that was adaptive to dynamic volatility expansion and contraction.

Bollinger Bands are a technical trading tool that is universal to all markets and trading time frames. This indicator was designed to show if prices are high or low on a relative basis for the chart.

Bollinger Bands consist of a middle band with two outer bands. The middle band is a simple moving average that is usually set at 20 periods. A simple moving average is used because the standard deviation formula also uses a simple moving average. The look-back period for the standard deviation is the same as for the simple moving average. The outer bands are usually set to two standard deviations above and below the middle band.

This indicator shows if price is high in relation to the upper band or if price is low in relation to the lower band. This information is valuable for both trading ranges and can show when a trend is about to emerge outside the bands. Volatility is based on the standard deviation, which changes as volatility increases and decreases. The bands automatically widen when volatility increases and contract when volatility decreases. Bollinger Bands are a good addition to a trader's charts and are useful inside the context of a confluence of other technical indicators. For example, if the lower Bollinger Band has a confluence with the 30 RSI it can have a higher probability as a dip buy signal.

A move in price to the upper band shows strength, while a price move to the lower band shows weakness. During range-bound markets and slow trends, price action will stay within the bounds of the bands. During strong uptrends, price will ride up the upper band and press it higher. During strong downtrends, the price will push against the lower band and force it lower. A break outside one end of the bands can be a parabolic trend signal in the direction of the breakout. In sideways markets price will revert from the upper or lower band to the middle 20-period moving average after reaching the top or the bottom band. If price is over the middle 20-period moving average it's signaling an upswing, and if price is below the 20-period moving average it's signaling a downswing.

John Bollinger has indicated that the bands should contain 88-89% of the price action on a chart, and a move outside the bands is a significant trend signal. Prices are high on a relative basis when above the upper band and low on a relative basis when below the lower band. Relatively high is not necessarily a bearish exit signal for long positions or a sell short signal, and relatively low is not necessarily a bullish buy signal. Prices can be high or low for a reason, sometimes that reason is due to a strong long-term trend in a market due to accumulation or distribution.

Bollinger Bands aren't meant to be used as a single trading tool, instead they are meant to be used on a chart within the full context of other technical indicators. Bollinger Bands are best used in correlation with other types of technical indicators to confirm key price levels on a chart, create good risk/reward ratios on entry and to help manage a trade for optimal exits.

*Note: Bollinger Bands® is a registered trademark of John Bollinger.

Chart created by Jake Wujastyk @Trendspider_J

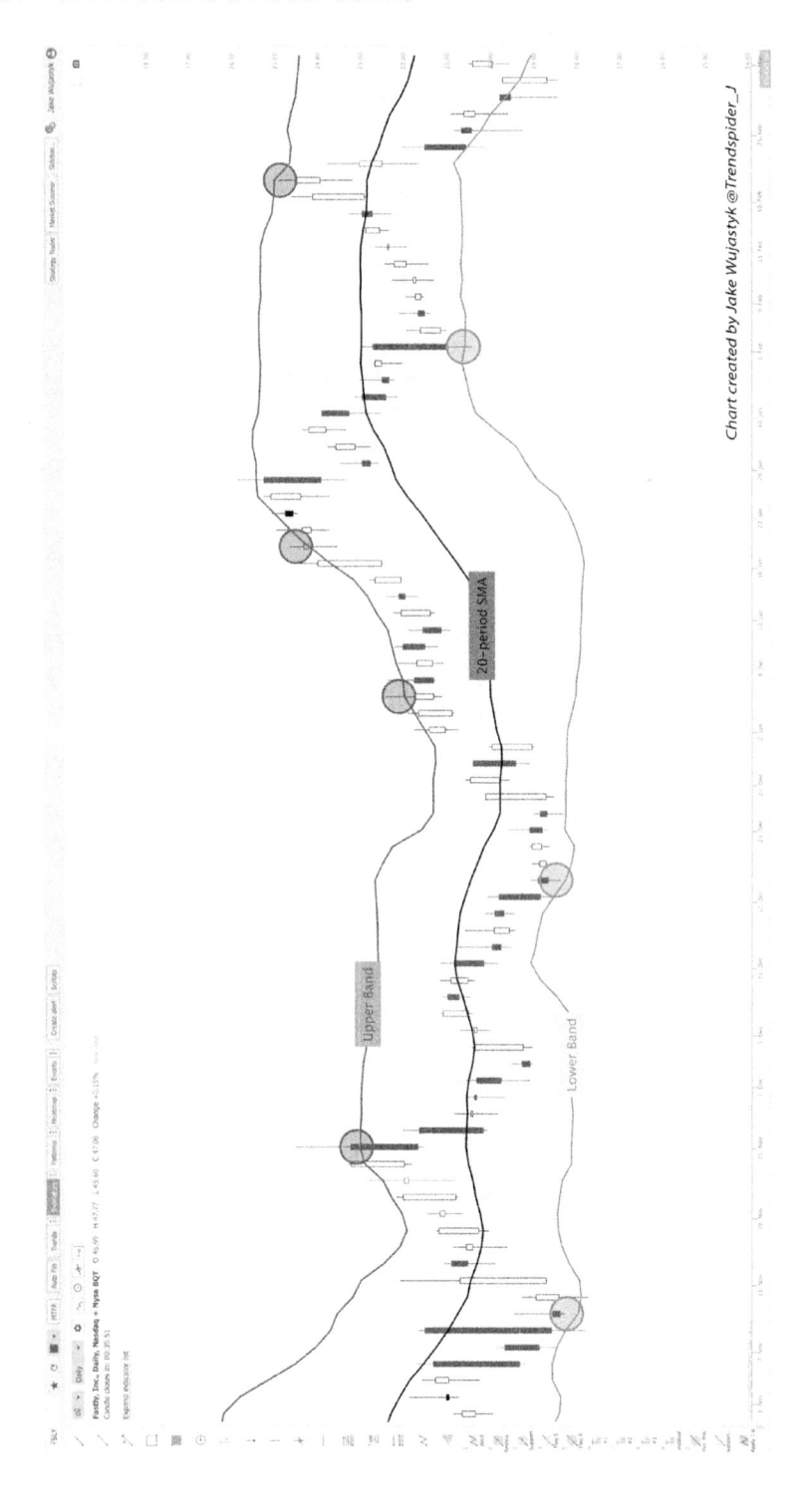

Average True Range

Average True Range (14) 4.784

What is the ATR? The average true range (ATR) indicator is the indicator used in technical analysis to quantify multi-day price range volatility on a chart. It's usually derived from the 14-day simple moving average of prices and trading range, and it calculates the full trading range of price action.

Charts can have gaps in price both up and down, and commodities and stock indexes can have price moves cut short when a limit is reached in a session. A volatility formula to track a price range on a chart that only uses the high and low of an intra-day trading range fails to capture volatility from both opening price gaps and limit moves. J. Welles Wilder created the *Average True Range* to quantify the missing volatility from the open to the close. The ATR is not a technical indicator of the direction of price action, it only focusses on the volatility on the chart. Wilder featured the ATR indicator in his 1978 book, *New Concepts in Technical Trading Systems*.

The average true range technical reading is calculated with the daily price range change and uses the greatest of three possible readings: high minus the previous close, previous close minus the low or the high minus the low.

$$\text{Current ATR} = [(\text{Prior ATR} \times 13) + \text{Current TR}] / 14$$

- Multiply the previous 14-day ATR by 13.
- Add the most recent day's TR value.
- Divide the total by 14.

The ATR can provide the multi-day range of price movement and help a trader position size based on time frame and chart volatility. One example of how to use the ATR is if the entry is $103 and your stop loss is the $100 price with a $1 ATR. You would have three days' worth of movement against you as your stop.

Start with your stop loss level and volatility on the chart to quantify your position size. The more room on your stop loss determines how big of a position size you can take. Your position size should be based on how much capital you are willing to lose if your stop loss is triggered. You can measure your risk in ATRs.

One type of trailing stop order uses the ATR indicator as a moving signal that expands as the trading range grows and contracts as the trading range gets smaller. This can also help to set position sizing based on the volatility risk of the current average true range.

For an ATR trailing stop, the 14-day period average ATR is commonly used. Here is an example of a multiple of 3-ATRs. These are plotted on the chart as a visual trailing stop to use to signal an exit to lock in existing profits when the price action moves down. In the case of a long position, the 3-ATR would be trailing below the price on the chart, and in the case of a short position the 3-ATR would be trailing above the price.

Chart courtesy of TrendSpider.com

The ATR can be used as a mechanical trailing stop order, removing the psychological pressure of discretionary decision making. The ATR can quantify where to set an initial stop-loss at entry and where to exit a winning trade based on a trailing stop.

The ATR is a moving indicator and changes with the degree of volatility in price action. It's wider in range in highly volatile charts and tighter in less volatile charts. A 2-ATR trailing stop can be used in extremely volatile markets to lower the risk of distance to the stop loss or trailing stop.

Using an ATR trailing stop starts at entry, and if price gets lower than the ATR multiple that was chosen from your entry price, you exit for a loss at that technical level. If your trade is a winner, then you exit the winning trade when it reverses lower than your ATR trailing stop.

Using an ATR trailing stop is a type of trend following system that allows your winners to run and cuts your losses short, while also giving room for a trade to work out without a premature exit. This is a mechanical way to manage your trade exits using the ATR indicator as a trailing stop order.

An ascending ATR that increases in value indicates that a chart has expanding volatility. A descending ATR that decreases in value shows a chart has contracting volatility. The directional move of the ATR indicates the current trend in volatility.

The ATR trailing stop is a risk management tool and exit signal used after an entry is taken, it doesn't act as an independent buy or sell signal. The ATR can also be used as a position sizing tool and a volatility filter to see the range in the current price action.

THE ULTIMATE GUIDE TO TECHNICAL ANALYSIS 89

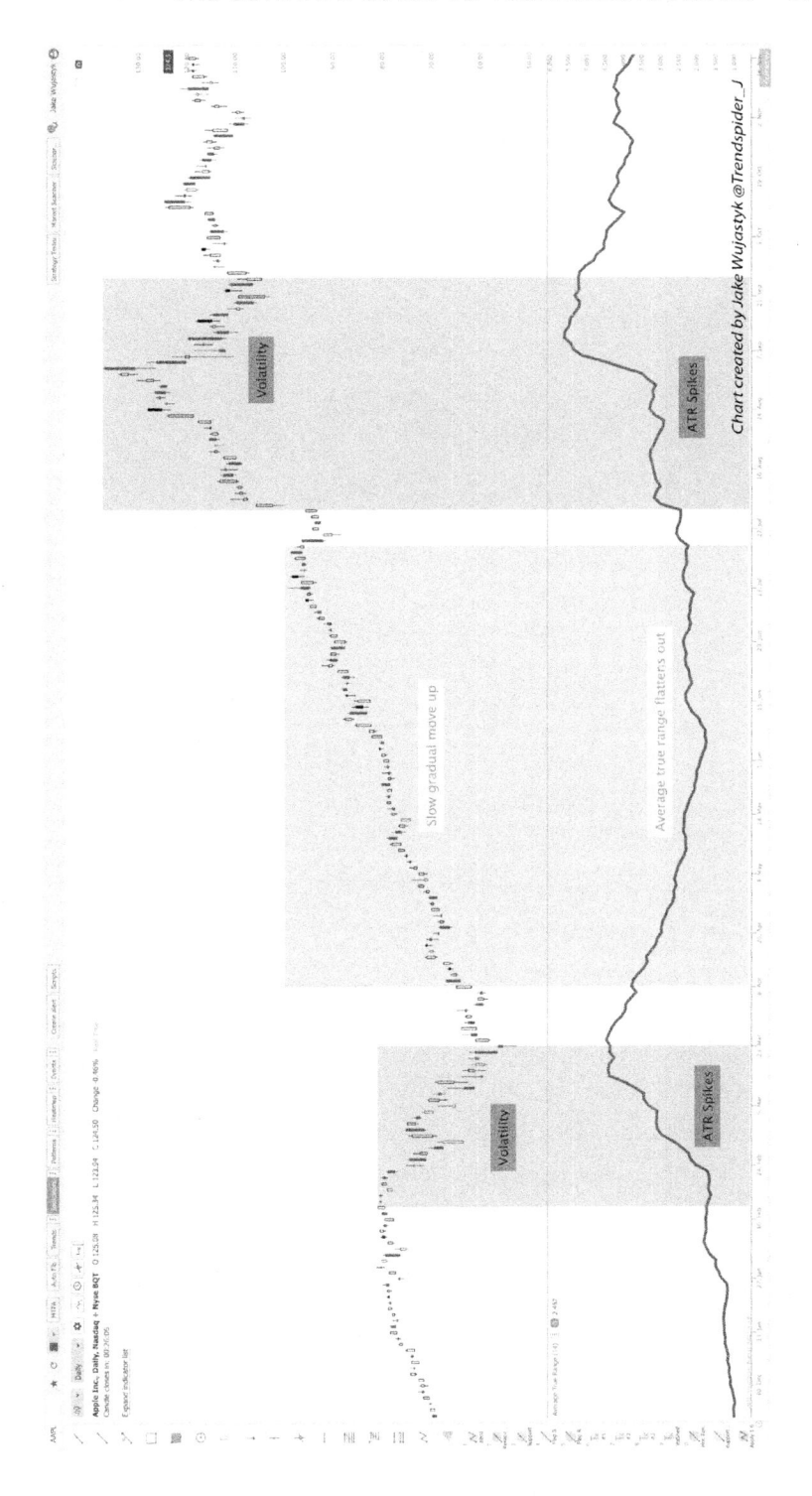

Standard Deviation

(chart showing +3 Standard Deviations, +2 Standard Deviations, +1 Standard Deviation, and Basis Moving Average (Standard Deviations are a function of this line))

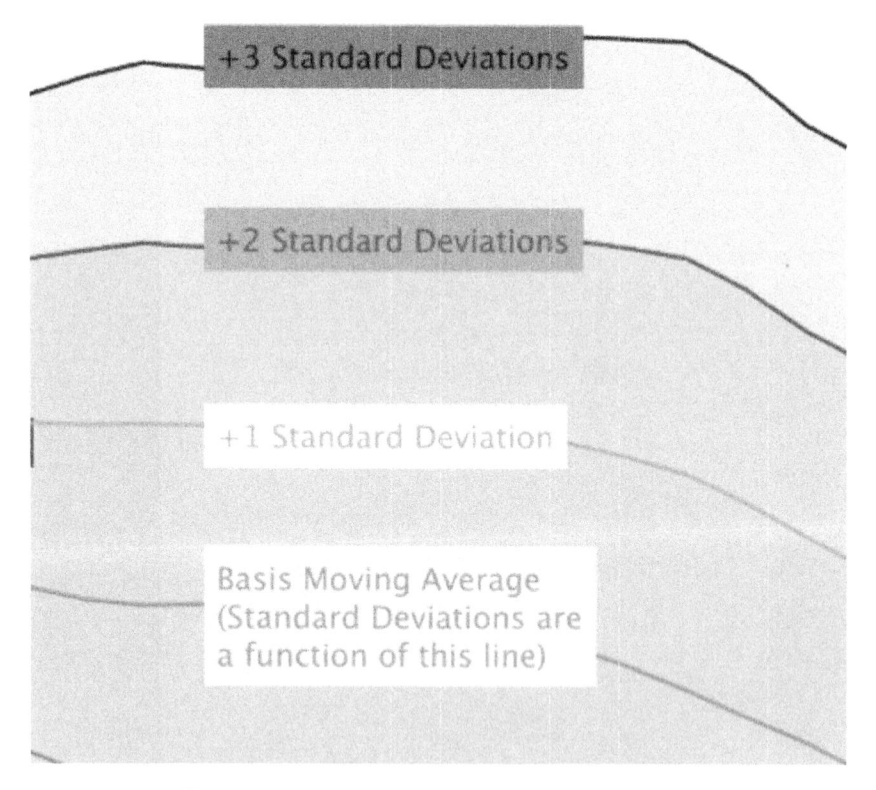

Charts created by Jake Wujastyk @Trendspider_J

IN STATISTICS, THE STANDARD DEVIATION IS A MEASUREMENT OF the magnitude of variation of a set of numbers that represent values some distance away from an original starting point. A smaller standard deviation shows that values are closer to the mean or average expectations of a set of data. A higher standard deviation shows that the values are more varied and over a larger range of possibilities extended from the average.

A standard deviation can also be represented in a formula with the Greek letter sigma 'σ' or simply with the Latin letter 's'.

In investing and trading, if price points are extended far from the average of prices, there's a higher standard deviation of asset prices. It's volatile and tends to move in a larger trading range.

A standard deviation is also a way to statistically measure the annual rate of return of a market or stock to see the historical volatility of that investment or trading vehicle.

A volatile market or speculative stock will tend to have a higher standard deviation of prices on average, while most big cap stocks and stock market indexes typically have a lower standard deviation and stay closer to historical prices.

Standard deviation is also used in risk management to measure the possible downside. It calculates all the volatility and uncertainty in both higher and lower prices as part of market risk. Price movement is measured as part of the risk of a standard deviation, whether it's in the investor's or trader's favor or not.

In trading and investing, the standard deviation is used to measure the volatility of price action in the context of a price range and the distance from a key moving average. Some of the most popular technical indicators used to measure the standard deviation of prices are Bollinger Bands and Keltner Channels.

The wider the distance between the bands or channels of these indicators from the center moving average, the more volatile the market is said to be. The more that current price pushes against the outer bands of these indicators, the stronger the trend in one direction becomes. The longer that price action stays extended to multiple standard deviations from the moving average, the greater the odds of an eventual return to the average becomes; this is called a *reversion to the mean*.

The narrower that Bollinger Bands or Keltner Channels become, and the more they contain current prices, the lower the volatility is on a chart. If price is close to its short-term moving averages, then the market currently has low volatility and in a tight trading range.

Standard deviation expands during volatile markets and contracts during calm markets. Fear and uncertainty are generally the drivers of expanded volatility in a markets price action.

Here is a quick overview for an understanding of a standard deviation chart data set. You can see how the examples of the data will fall within one standard deviation of the mean for approximately 68% of the data set, staying within two standard deviations happens with approximately 95% of the data set sampled, and all the data samples typically fall within three standard deviations approximately 99.7% of the time.

The standard deviation identified on the chart as σ (the Greek letter sigma) is the square root of the variance of X, this is the square root of the average value of $(X - \mu)^2$. The standard deviation of a probability distribution is the same as that of a random variable having that distribution. A move of a 3-sigma event is three standard deviations from the mean.

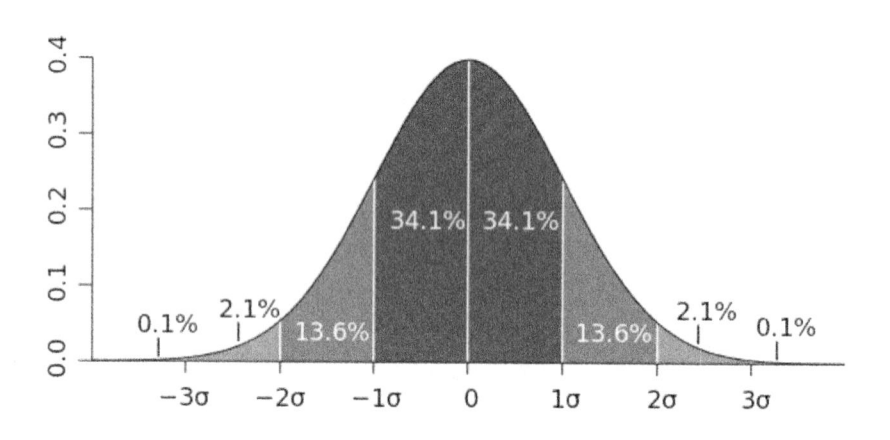

M. W. Toews / CC BY (https://creativecommons.org/licenses/by/2.5)

For traders and investors looking at the probabilities of price changes as they are usually distributed within the parameters of a classic bell curve, approximately 68% of price action will be within one standard deviation of the mean, approximately 95% will be contained within two standard deviations of the mean, and approximately 99.7% will happen inside three standard deviations of the mean. With these parameters of deviations, traders and investors can see the magnitude of a price movement away from the normal value zone for the time frame of a market. If price moves more than one standard deviation, it indicates that strength or weakness is greater than the average in the direction of the price movement and trend.

Trend traders look for outsized moves of a magnitude of three or more deviations from the mean that happen more than expected. When a large move happens, it can create significant winning trades and investments. These large, outsized moves occur more than expected and are called *Fat Tail* or *Black Swan* events. Due to the large sample size of financial markets, many moves happen every year greater than 3-sigma. Large unexpected moves can create huge wins or big losses depending on directional trades, position sizing, and how the trade is managed during the move.

Bollinger Bands and Keltner Channels are technical trading tools for measuring standard deviations with *envelopes* plotted on a chart. Technical indicators that create price envelopes show visual upper and lower standard deviations from an average of price. Two parameters are used; 20-period averages with two standard deviations are set as default values but can be adjusted for time frames or for a larger or smaller deviation.

The indicator bands adjust to volatility swings in the underlying price by expanding and contracting. These technical measurements are primarily used for reversion to the mean trades. They typically quantify how far price has pulled away from a key moving average, what the odds are of a return to the value zone back to the middle-line moving average.

Think of price like it's a rubber band being stretched farther and farther away from its starting point at the 20-day moving average.

Two things can happen as price stretches two, and then three deviations away from its value zone in the center of the envelope.

- The rubber band can snap back to the starting point which typically happens after the 3rd deviation level is reached. When a chart is sold short after the upper 3rd deviation line is reached on a chart and covered on a retracement back to the 20-period moving average, it's considered a reversion to the mean trade. A reversion to the mean trade would also be buying a dip as price dropped to the lower 3rd deviation line on a chart. In that case, the trade is betting on the probability of a return to the value zone.
- The other possibility is that the rubber band breaks, and price keeps going in a trend outside the normal 2nd and 3rd deviation envelopes from the 20-period moving average. This is considered a parabolic trend outside normal price action. It's rare in occurrence but can create large wins due to the magnitude of the move.

Standard deviations give a larger perspective on where price action is in relation to the 20-period moving average value zone, and how far way it has moved from a normal trading range. Most of the time, the risk/reward ratio for a directional trade diminishes as price reaches the 3rd deviation from the 20-period moving average, and the odds of pullback to the center line increases. Many strong trends will occur inside two deviations and lose momentum as they reach the 2nd line of the envelopes.

THE ULTIMATE GUIDE TO TECHNICAL ANALYSIS 95

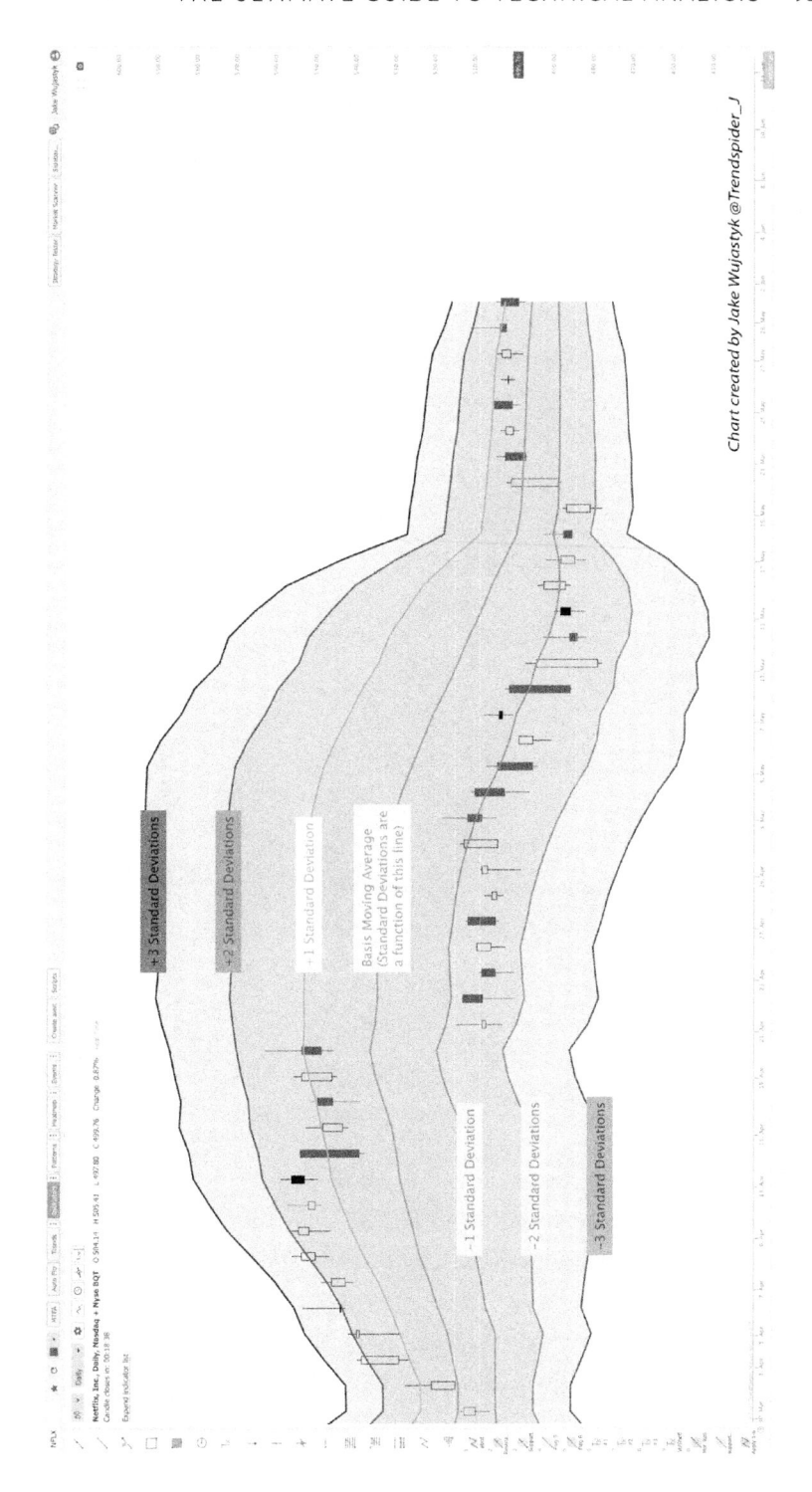

Chart created by Jake Wujastyk @Trendspider_J

16

TECHNICAL VOLUME INDICATORS

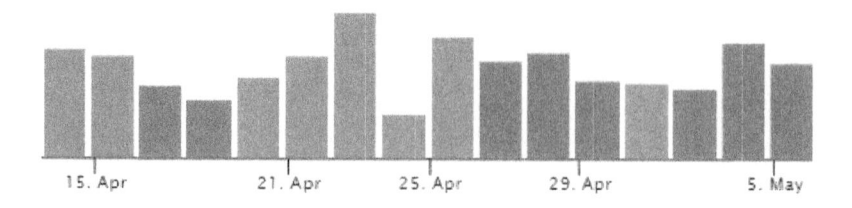

Volume as an Indicator

Volume is like votes on the price of a stock as each trade is an agreement between a buyer and a seller to exchange shares. The volume is the number of trades that occur during each period on a chart. Technical traders look for correlations between price action trends and the increasing and decreasing of volume.

Volume is the quantity of stock shares that trades between buyers and sellers during each candlestick or bar on a chart. Volume can be measured on any time frame from the one minute, to the hour, or on the daily or weekly chart. Stock trading volume on the daily chart would be the number of shares traded from the open of the day to the close of the day. The volume of trading and the changes to the amount of volume over time, can be important technical inputs for traders.

Liquidity can be the most important fundamental for a chart. Without volume making a market liquid enough to trade most other technical analysis doesn't matter. Volume is needed both from buyers and sellers to keep the bid/ask spreads tight for good order fills. A trader wants to focus on active names so they can have speed in the fills for their buy and sell orders. The farther a trader moves from the most active stocks and the major exchanges the slower and wider their fills will become. On the options market the farther a trader gets from the front month options in time or the at-the-money options in price the less liquid an option contract will be for trading.

Volume is what creates technical levels as buyers wait at support levels to buy and sellers wait to distribute at resistance levels on a chart. Downtrends occur when there is a lack of buyers at key price levels, so sellers must go searching to be filled at lower prices to exit. Uptrends occur when there is a lack of sellers at higher price levels, so buyers must go searching at higher prices to find sellers willing to exit their shares by selling to them. Don't get confused, buyers and sellers are always equal in every trade transaction on a chart, but it is the price that changes on where they agree to let a stock change ownership.

Volume is one of the most important technical indicators for analysis because it is used to quantify the strength of a price move. The higher the volume during a swing or trend in price action, the more valid the move usually is. The lower the volume during a swing or trend in price action, the less valid the move could be.

Volume can be an indicator of accumulation or distribution on a chart. Uptrends should see rising or steady volume on higher prices to validate the trend. Buying pressure pushes prices higher showing accumulation and buying and holding for the stock increasing. Downtrends should see rising volume on lower prices to validate the trend. Selling pressure pushes prices lower showing distribution and people exiting a stock. Breakouts from a price range have more validation and meaning when they occur on a higher-than-average volume.

Volume is primarily used to confirm a price move in technical analysis. Traders look for a confluence between higher volume and higher prices and higher volume and lower prices. Bearish divergences between volume and price action occur when a stock chart makes a higher high in prices on lower than usual volume. Bullish divergences between volume and price action occur when a stock chart makes a lower low in prices on lower than usual volume. Both these divergences could signal a reversal in price action from the current trend. High volume confirms price action while low volume shows there is little conviction in a move.

A large reversal in price action from the current trend along with a large increase in volume can signal a high probability that the current trend has ended, and the next move could be in the opposite direction or sideways. Many times, a reversal in a trend will show a large reversal candle on a chart that ends in the opposite direction of the current trend along with a large spike in volume. On a chart reversal the volume can start with a large spike then the volume can decrease as the trend reversal plays out.

On days when price ends higher volume can be marked green and considered bullish. On days when price ends lower volume can be marked red and considered bearish. This classification means the volume on that day was primarily one sentiment even though all the trades were not necessarily bullish or bearish just that the move was primarily in one direction.

Volume is the fuel for price moves and can be a warning sign of the possible failure of a move when a trend in volume doesn't confirm the trend in price action. Volume shows the votes for a specific price range on chart. Low volume shows low support and high volume shows high support for the correlating price action on the chart. A

THE ULTIMATE GUIDE TO TECHNICAL ANALYSIS 99

trade has a higher probability of success when it is confirmed by volume.

Chart courtesy of TrendSpider.com

Vertical volume bars measures volume by price instead of time periods. The TrendSpider.com charting platform has an Anchored Volume-by-Price setting that shows what price levels experienced the most volume. Unlike traditional volume that's plotted on the X-axis below the price chart, price-by-volume is plotted on the Y-Axis on the right side of the chart, with each bar representing the volume at the associated price. The further the volume bar is from the right of the screen; the more volume was traded at that level.

Volume-by-Price is helpful for identifying important price levels where a lot of traders have placed trades.

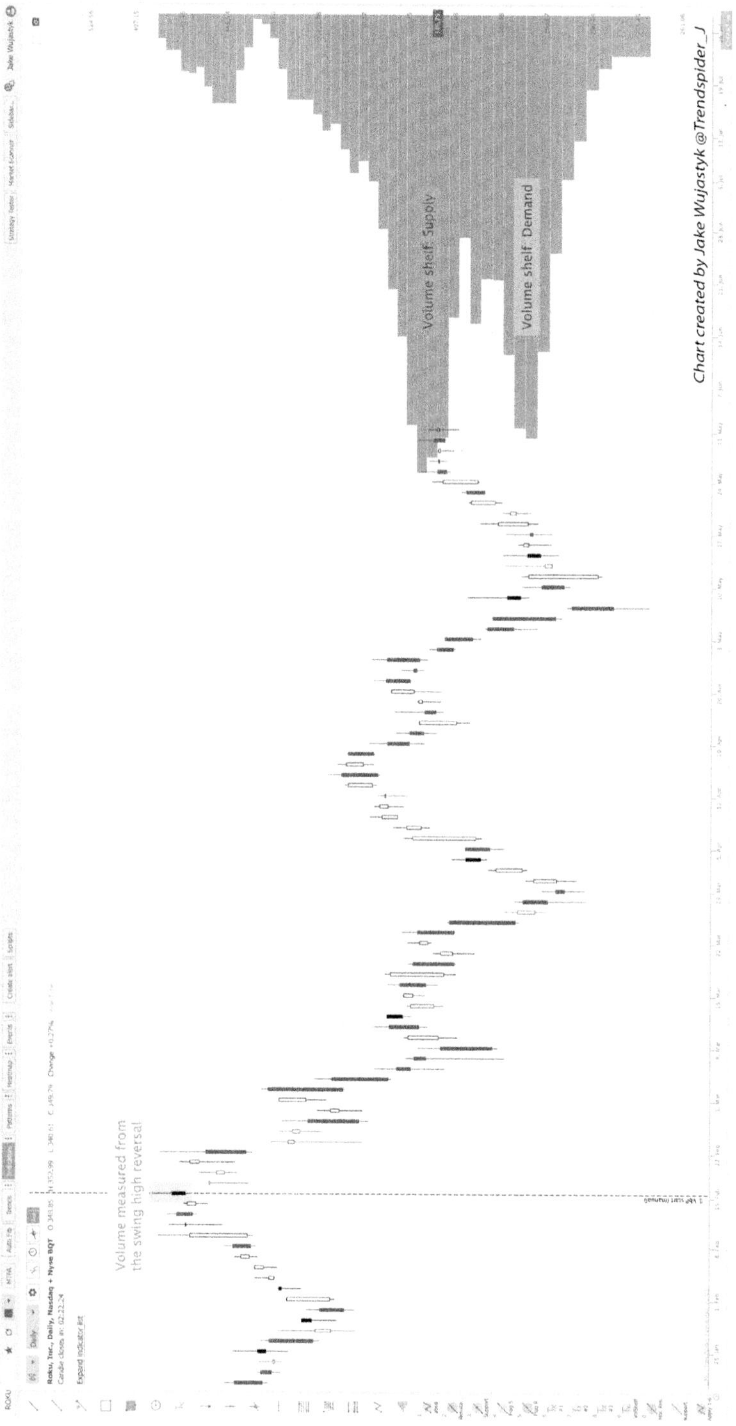
Volume shelf: Supply
Volume shelf: Demand
Volume measured from the swing high reversal
Chart created by Jake Wujastyk @Trendspider_J

Chaikin Money Flow

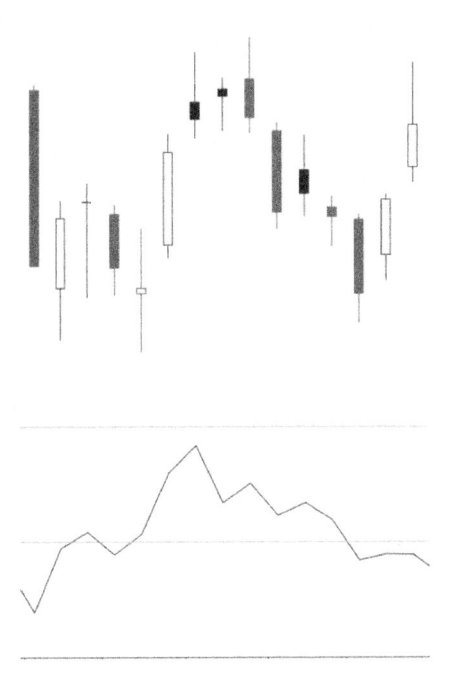

The Chaikin Money Flow or CMF is a technical indicator created by Marc Chaikin and is a volume-weighted average of accumulation and distribution over a specific period. The standard period used for this indicator is 20 days and is usually the default setting on many charting platforms.

The CMF quantifies money flow volume over a chosen look-back period. The Chaikin Money Flow value fluctuates between 1 and -1 around its zero line.

The concept behind the Chaikin Money Flow is when its reading is near the high of the period, it shows a greater amount of accumulation happened. Also, when the closing reading is near the low, a greater amount of distribution happened. If price action consistently closes higher than the price range midpoint on increasing volume, the

Chaikin Money Flow is positive. Also, when the price action consistently closes lower than the price range midpoint on increasing volume, the Chaikin Money Flow will be negative.

If CMF is positive and closer to +1, buying pressure is greater.

If CMF is negative and closer to -1, selling pressure is greater.

Buying pressure can confirm a current uptrend will continue. Selling pressure can confirm a current downtrend will continue. This can give the trader a confluence signal between both price and volume showing a higher probability that a current trend will continue.

During an uptrend, continuing buying pressure with CMF values above 0 can signal prices will continue to go higher.

During a downtrend, continuing selling pressure with CMF values below 0 can signal prices will continue to go lower.

When CMF crosses the zero line in either direction, this can be a signal that a trend reversal could be close. The CMF value above the zero line is a signal of price strength on the chart, and a value below the zero line is a signal of weakness on the chart.

How to use the CMF indicator for trading:

Bullish crosses occur when CMF crosses from below the zero line to above the zero line.

Bearish crosses occur when CMF crosses from above the zero line to back below the zero line.

The CMF can be used as a technical indicator to confirm a breakout of price action in either direction by using trendlines or support and resistance lines on the CMF indicator in relation to price action. If price breaks out above resistance on the chart it can be confirmed by the CMF when it also has a positive value confirming the direction of the breakout.

A bearish divergence CMF sell signal is triggered when price action has a higher high with an overbought reading and the CMF diverges with a lower high and begins going lower.

A bullish divergence CMF buy signal is triggered when price

action has a lower low with an oversold reading and the CMF diverges with a higher low and begins going higher.

Chart courtesy of TrendSpider.com

On-Balance Volume OBV

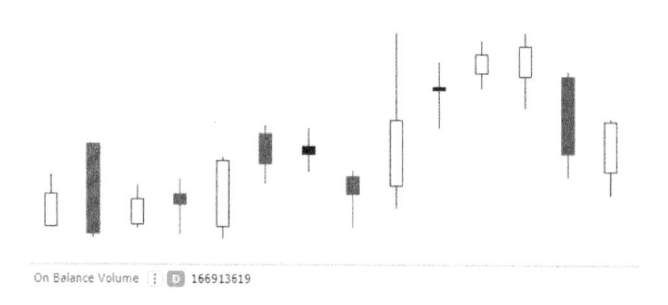

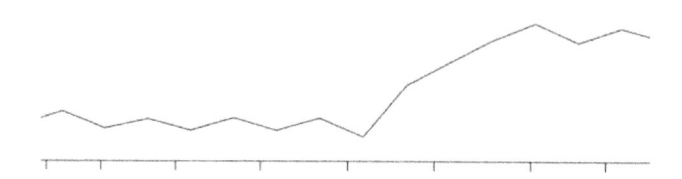

On-Balance Volume (OBV) is a type of momentum indicator that uses volume to project the potential for price change. It measures buying and selling pressure as a cumulative indicator. By adding up the volume on up days and subtracting volume on down days, the indicator calculates and quantifies when the market is showing accumulation and when it's showing distribution on a chart independent of pure price action alone. Volume may show something different happening underneath the actual price action or it could confirm the current trend.

OBV was created by Joe Granville and shared in his 1963 book, "Granville's New Key to Stock Market Profits." This was one of the first technical indicators to measure positive and negative volume flow on a chart. Technical traders can see divergences between OBV and price action to project price movement probabilities or use the OBV to confirm a trend currently underway on a chart.

The On-Balance Volume (OBV) line on a chart is the running total of positive and negative volume. A time period's volume is positive when the close is above the prior closing price and is negative when the close is below the prior closing price. This can be applied to any time frame to see the flow of volume in correlation to the trend of price action.

Granville believed that volume comes before prices. OBV increases when volume on up days is more than volume on down days. OBV decreases when volume on down days is higher. An ascending OBV shows positive volume pressure that can project higher prices. The inverse is a descending OBV that shows negative volume pressure that can project lower prices. Granville saw through his own research that OBV would many times move before price action followed. Price should move higher if OBV is increasing. Prices can either stay flat or are even move lower early in an OBV move higher. Price should move lower if OBV is decreasing but prices could remain flat or even keep moving higher early with this signal.

The actual value of OBV isn't an important factor. Technical traders need to focus their attention on the trend and momentum of the OBV line itself. Defining the directional trendline for OBV is the most important factor in using it. Observe whether the current trend of OBV is the same trend for the underlying stock or trading vehicle on the chart. Look for key support or resistance levels. Once broken the trend for OBV could change and these breakouts could be used as new trend signals.

OBV is based on the closing prices of the chosen time frame. Closing prices should be what is considered when analyzing divergences or support/resistance breakouts. Large increases in volume can at times distort the indicator by causing a large sudden move that will take time to average out in the OBV indicator.

Bullish and bearish divergence signals on the OBV versus price action can signal a high probability of a trend reversal happening. These signals are based on the belief that the volume on a chart will indicate the direction of the next price move. A bullish divergence happens when OBV moves higher or has a higher low at the same time prices move lower or form a lower low. A bearish divergence happens when OBV moves lower or creates a lower low as prices move higher or form a higher high. The divergence between OBV and price action should signal technical traders that a reversal in price action could soon follow.

OBV is a leading indicator that shows the strength of current volume in correlation with the directional move of price action. Big volume increases can impact this indicator reading for the period used. Other technical indicators should be used in correlation with OBV to get a more complete picture of volume and price action as this is just one metric on a chart.

THE ULTIMATE GUIDE TO TECHNICAL ANALYSIS 107

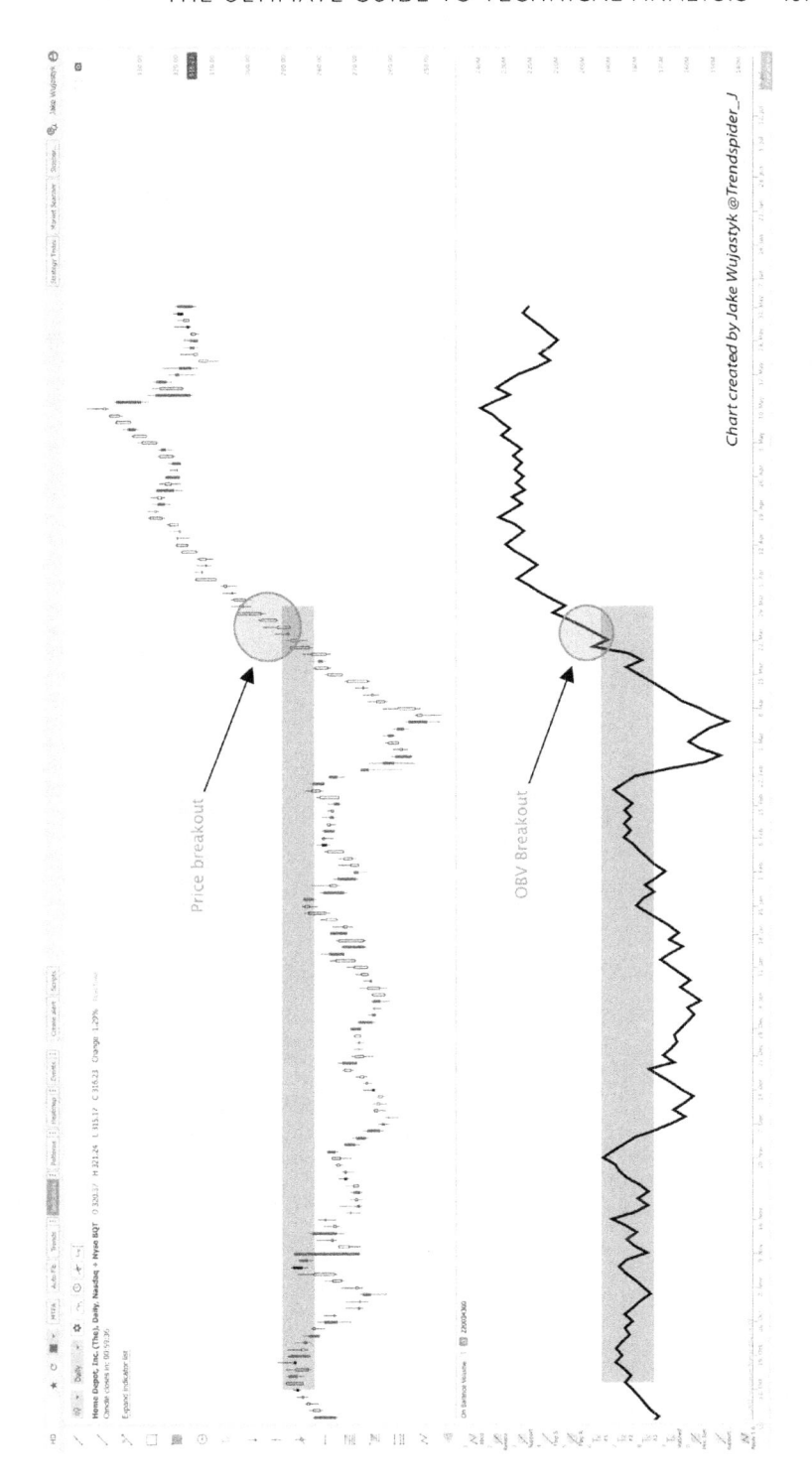

Chart created by Jake Wujastyk @Trendspider_J

Relative Volume Indicator (RVOL) on the TrendSpider Platform

A trader can use this indicator on the TrendSpider.com platform to quickly scan any index or sector list to find stocks that have above-average volume rates in seconds.

Relative volume is calculated by taking the ratio of current volume relative to an average. It gives you a quick way to see how much volume is relative to a period and which direction it is pointing in.

Features:

- Customizable average (type and period).
- Customizable base level.
- Area-plot chart visualization.
- Full support for multi-time frame analysis.
- Fully supported in TrendSpider's market scanner, strategy tester, and multi-factor alert system.
- How to add it to your charts:
- Add Relative Volume (RVOL) in the Indicator Manager.
- Configure your moving average (default length = 20, default type = SMA). This will calculate the moving average of the volume level to measure relativity against.
- Select your base level. This is the midpoint on the relative volume chart.
- Customize your colors.
- Apply changes.

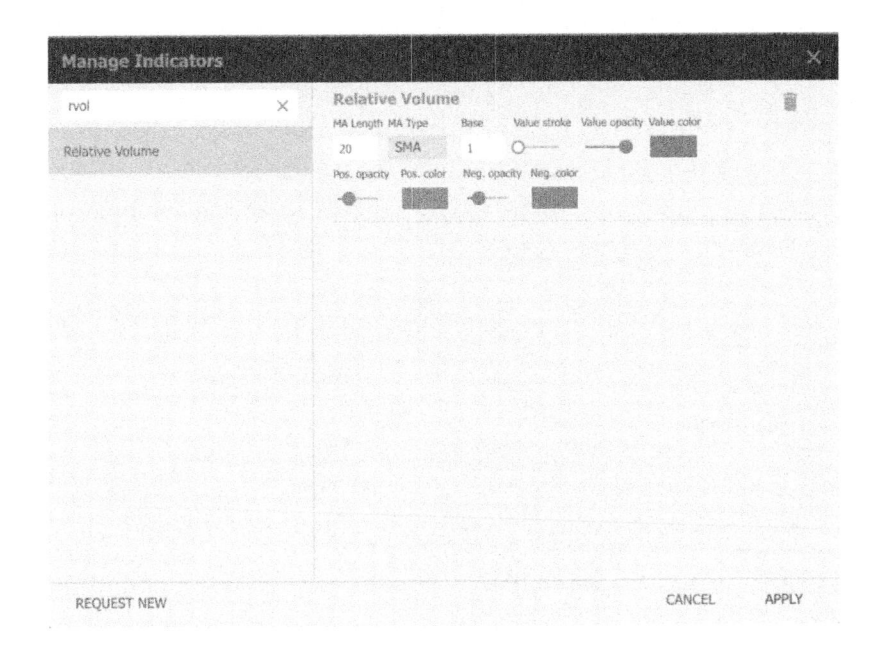

How it works:

When added to your chart, the volume level relative to the base you select will be displayed as an area plot. The below two charts show the same RVOL indicator, with the top one's base set to 2 and the bottom chart's base set to 3. This moves the base level higher and causes fewer spikes. This is a great way to measure volume relative to a past period average (in this case a 20-period simple average.)

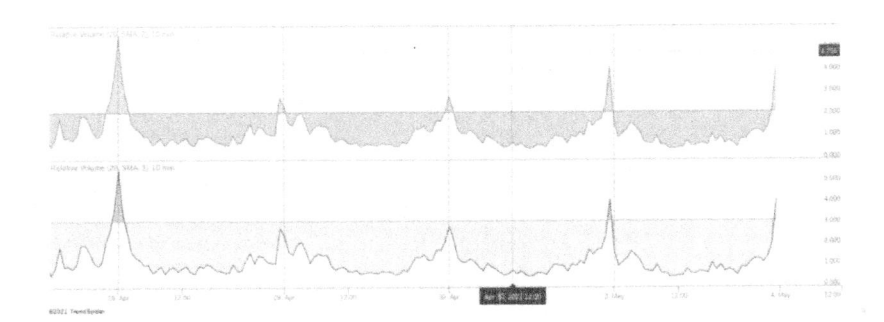

When you enable multi-time frame Analysis with RVOL, you will see something like this chart (below.) Here you can see there are now two bands on the chart instead of one. The dashed band is from the 1-hour time frame, while the solid bands are from the 10-minute time frame. This allows you to look at relative volume across multiple time frames in a single indicator.

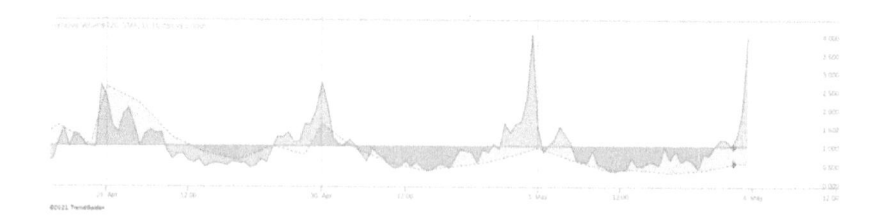

How to use it in the Market Scanner, Strategy Tester and Multi-Factor Alert scripts:

Using the Market Scanner, you can search an index, say the Russell 2000, for stocks with high relative volume. In this example by searching the Russell 2000 for any stock that has a relative volume over 3. This yields stocks that have an abnormally large spike in volume occurring on them. This is where TrendSpider's unique *Current Candle* option comes in. Using this option, you can scan for conditions while they are happening on any time frame, instead of waiting for the candle to close as with many other scanning tools. This capability is useful when using RVOL in scanners because you can catch the move as it is starting instead of when it is ending.

Using RVOL in scanners with multiple time periods and other indicators

RVOL can be used in combination with other indicators in your Scanning, Backtesting and Alerting conditions, in this example, two separate time frames are used for RVOL (1 hour and Daily) as well as a 90 minute .

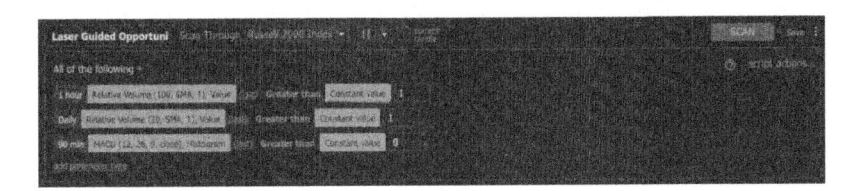

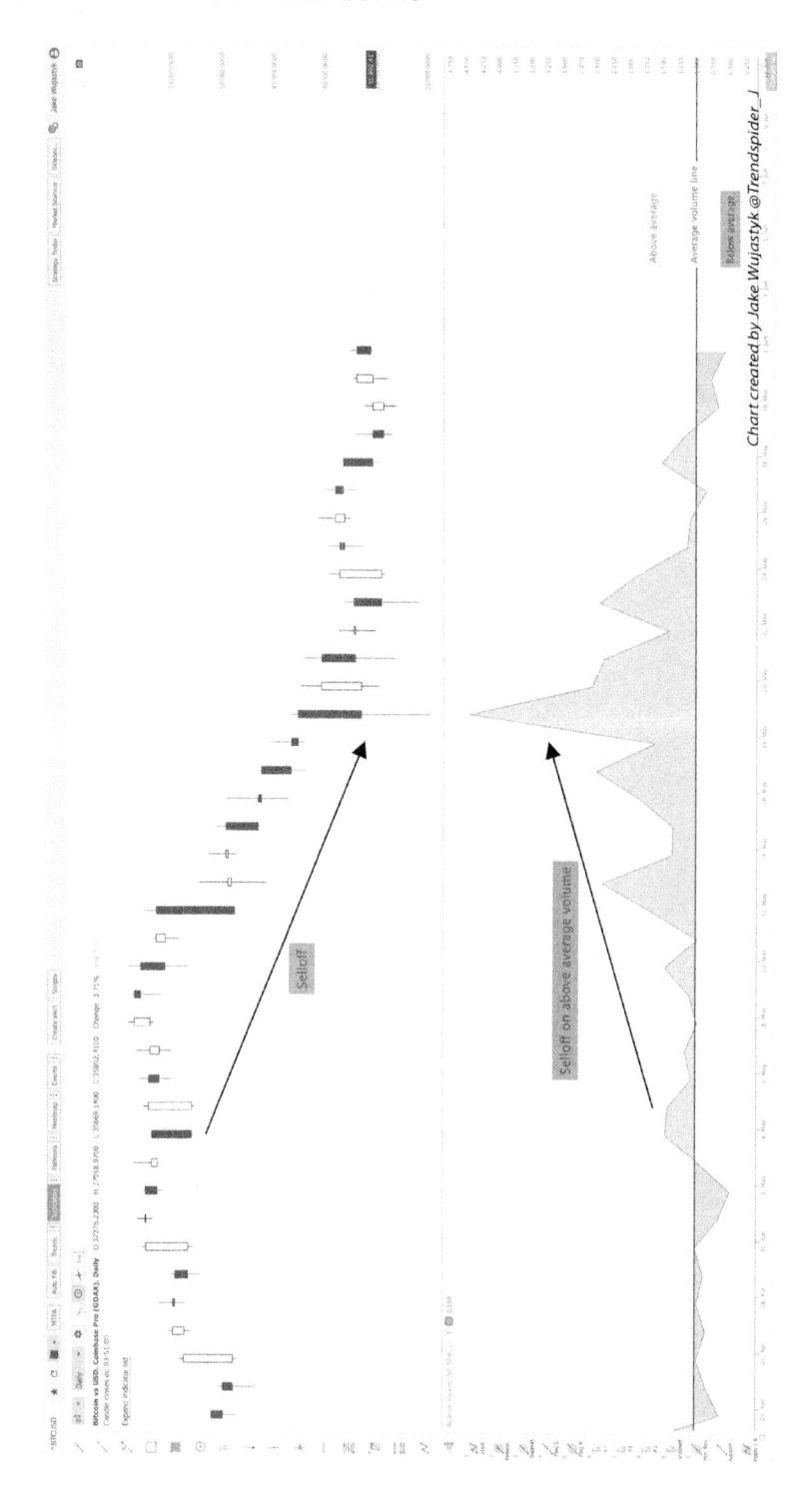

17

DIVERGENCES

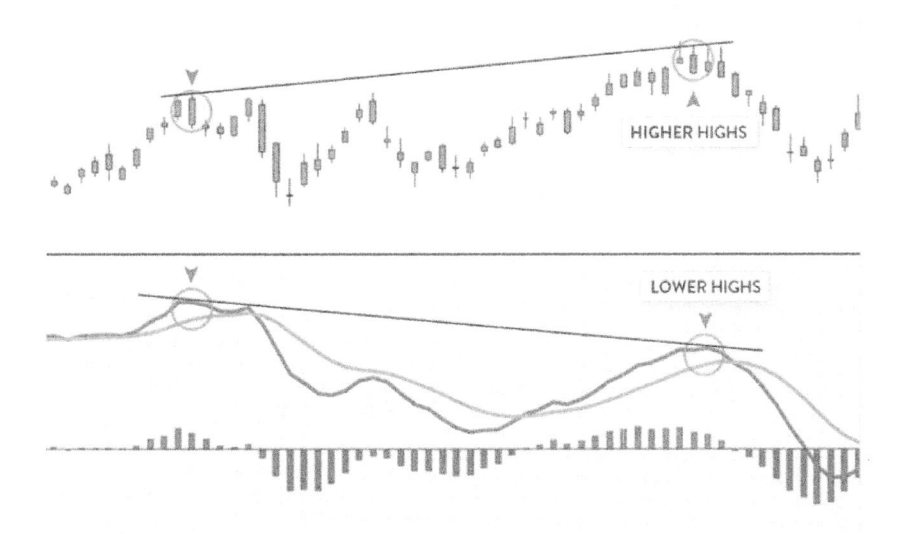

A bullish divergence is identified by prices making new lower lows or higher highs without a technical indicator, like an oscillator, making a new, correlated low or high. This is a signal that the current price sentiment is losing momentum with a high probability that there will be a reversal from the current trend in the market. A divergence is a signal that a chart may be near a bottom or top for the chosen time frame.

In many instances, a bullish divergence can be the key indicator that signals the end of a downtrend, and that the risk/reward ratio has shifted in favor of the bulls. A bearish divergence can be the key indicator on a chart that signals the end of an uptrend, and that the risk/reward ratio has shifted in the favor of the bears.

Technical oscillators used to find divergences include the popular Relative Strength Index (RSI) and the Moving Average Convergence-Divergence (MACD), among others. The RSI not only measures the extremes of overbought (70) or oversold (30), but also shows divergences between it making lower lows and price not making lower lows. The MACD can signal bullish or bearish crosses and also its divergence with price action.

The RSI or MACD can be used to filter price action and momentum, but they can also be used to compare price as traders look at the direction of the indicator's momentum versus the trend in price action. The divergence between the technical indicator and the price movement can signal changes in a trend and the probabilities of a reversal on a chart.

A bullish divergence is signaled when prices move lower but an oscillator moves higher. This is a valid technical signal to go long based on technical analysis. This indicates a high probability but isn't always accurate, so proper position sizing is still required and stop losses must be used to limit losses. Remember that the profitability is not in the entry but rather it's in the exit. You should have a strategy in place to maximize and lock in profits if it does work out as a winning trade. An exit can be planned when an overbought reading (70 RSI area) is reached for a long trade, or a short trade exited when an oversold reading (30 RSI area) is reached. These are two potential types of profit targets that could be used. Another option is using a short-term moving average like the 10-day EMA as a trailing stop after an entry.

Divergences signal a shifting of both momentum in the current trend and a change in the risk/reward ratio for open trades in the direction of the current trend. Divergences are a great way to combine both price action and technical indicators to analyze a chart through two filters. It allows you to see when they begin to disagree about the strength of the current sentiment and what is the true path of least resistance.

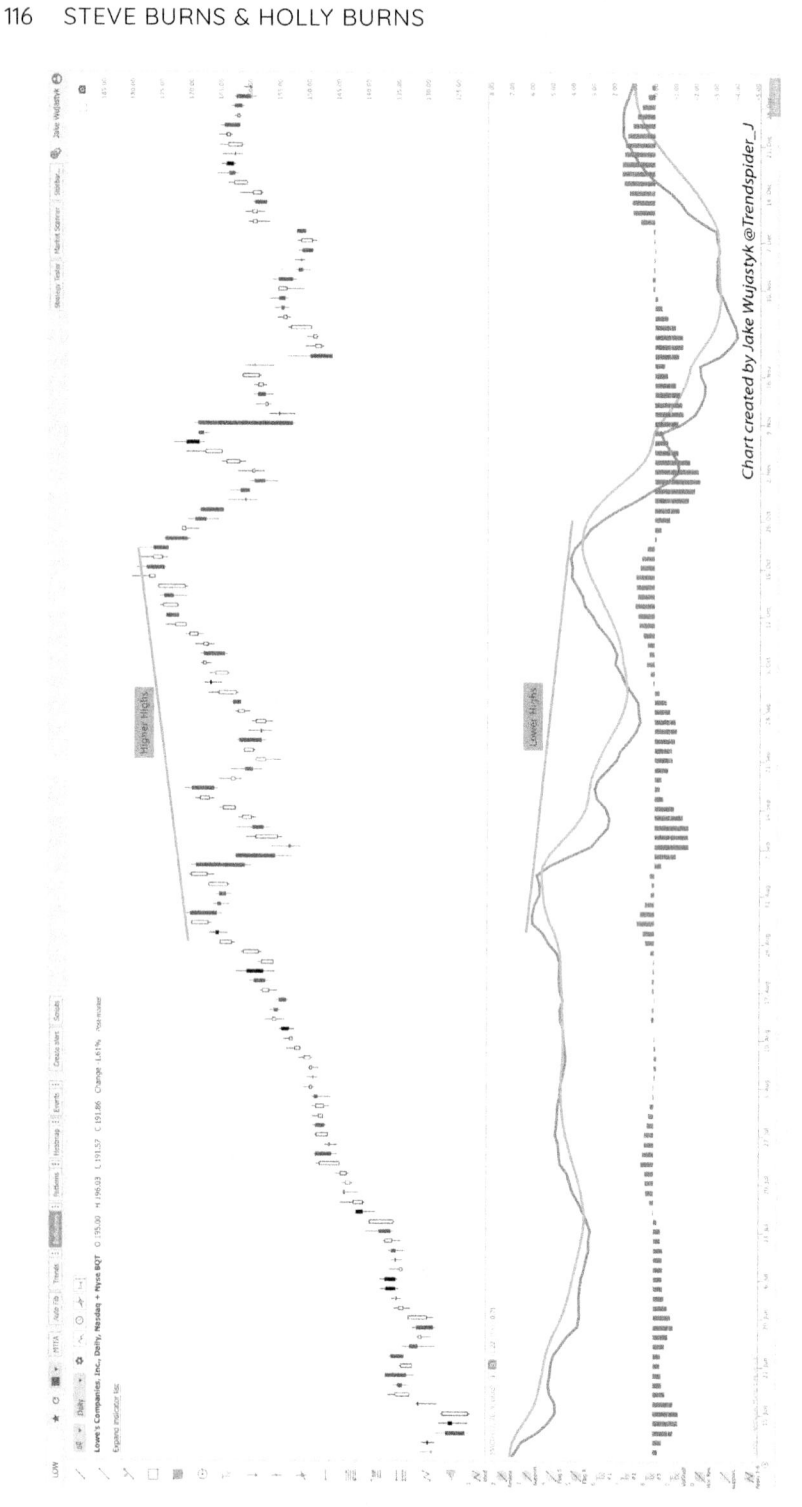

THE ULTIMATE GUIDE TO TECHNICAL ANALYSIS 117

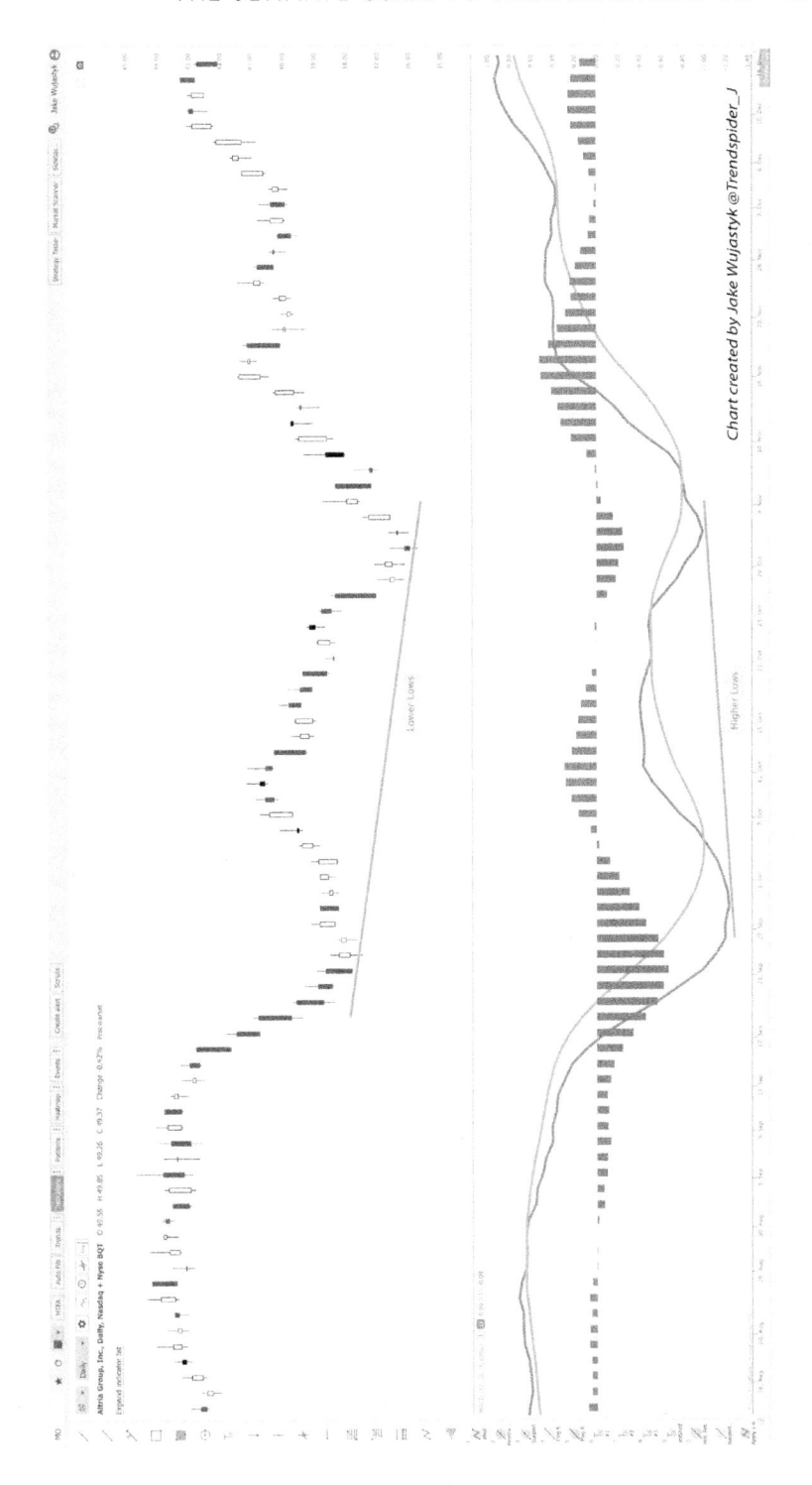

18

COMMON MISTAKES IN TECHNICAL ANALYSIS

There are some common mistakes people make in the practice of technical analysis, and in this chapter, I'll outline some of these challenges and discuss ways to avoid them on your trading journey.

There are two types of technical analysis, predictive technical analysis and reactive technical analysis. Predictive analysis attempts to map out what the market will do in the future based on the current pattern on a chart. Reactive technical analysis uses current signals in price action to signal good buy and sell decisions based on optimum risk/reward ratios that go in the direction of the current momentum and trend.

A common mistake made by many people unfamiliar with the application of technical analysis is not understanding the dynamics of win rate, risk management and watchlist selection. Technical analysis is a tool for putting the odds in your favor when trading price action. It can show the path of least resistance and give a trader price levels to set stop losses and profit targets that create good risk/reward ratios.

Technical analysis is not a magical system or 100% accurate in predicting future price action, but it is a way to examine price action to analyze current patterns and future possibilities. Technical analysis is an attempt to move away from opinions and predictions and quantify what a chart's price action is doing. It's a way to stop focusing on what you wish would happen and start focusing on what is happening. Many traders mistakenly analyze a chart and then turn that historical analysis into a belief in the future. A chart is always changing and evolving and reactive technical analysis updates with new data.

Support and resistance only matter in a trading range, once there is a breakout in one direction of the horizontal range, it's no longer valid because the chart has transitioned from trading in a range to a trend. Uptrends have no long-term resistance and downtrends have no long-term support because a real trend will keep making new directional highs or lows based on its direction as long as it lasts. When a chart stops breaking to new price levels, it's a signal that the trend may have ended in that time frame. A chartist must have the flexibility to see the change in price dynamics and not get locked into one belief.

At the beginning of a trend, a chart will shift from support and resistance being a horizontal range to a vertical range where moving averages and trendlines come into play. The trader should see this change in market dynamics as their trend signals start getting triggered, like breakouts and moving average crossovers. A trend can't be traded the same way you would trade in a range-bound market.

Thinking that *it will bounce back, it can't go any higher* or *I'll just hold until my trade gets back to even*, are some of the biggest mistakes a trader can make. It demonstrates that they have shifted from using technical analysis to relying on hope. Traders that use technical analysis focus on math and signals for entries and exits, while emotional traders rely on feelings of hope, desire and fear.

Moving averages are useful tools for trading trends but become less dependable in trading ranges and highly volatile markets. A trading system must account for the level of volatility on a chart through position sizing and situational awareness. A breakout in price action that happens at an extremely overbought area on a chart like the 70 RSI, may not have the same quality risk/reward ratio as one that happens in the area around the 50 RSI.

Cognitive bias is dangerous for any trader. If you believe too much in any narrative or become too bearish or bullish, it can create a cognitive bias that results in you only seeing what you want to see to confirm your own belief system.

Overbought and oversold indicators fail to be meaningful in parabolic trends. A strongly trending market can continue to be overbought or oversold. A stop loss is a tool to keep losses small when technical analysis fails on a chart. Position sizing is the safety net that saves a trading account from ruin when Black Swans move markets beyond traditional boundaries. Anything can happen in the market at any time, which is why risk must always be managed.

Technical analysis is not the same on every time frame and on every chart. You can see different patterns on intraday, daily, weekly and monthly charts, so it's important to focus on the time frame your trade is taking place in. Also, different markets and stocks have different price patterns and volatility levels. You must know the historical characteristics of your chart. A speculative growth stock is not going to move in the same way that a big cap stock does. Likewise, a traditional forex currency pair is not going to move the same as a cryptocurrency. Know your markets behavioral price action patterns before you start trading it. Historical chart studies and backtesting can expand your knowledge before you start trading.

Some people who mistakenly try to disprove technical trading practices don't realize that they have no filters in place. They try to backtest signals on a large sample of stocks with no understanding of how different they are, and they don't filter for volatility. They try to be 100% mechanical in their backtesting without first being discretionary in designing the best way to backtest for a system with an edge. They don't understand the edge that comes in reactive trade management in real-time with moving stop losses to trailing stops or selling into strength during an overbought reading on a chart. They don't understand how to program a purely mechanical system with an edge, or how they can manage trades as they play out with discretionary rules, so they denounce trading price action is a scam. There are plenty of millionaire and billionaire traders that disagree with them.

Technical analysis must be flexible, and as a pattern or trend changes, a trader must change their interpretation. 90% of technical analysis is determining which direction a price is breaking out, the other 10% is narrative.

Technical analysis is best used as a tool for profitable trading. The best way to be profitable in the markets is to have small losses and large wins. Technical analysis can help create good risk/reward ratios by looking at important price levels. It can also help you place a trade in the direction of least resistance for a better chance of catching a trend. Everything else is just opinions and predictions. The mistake is believing technical analysis is predictive of the future when it's really a tool to analyze the possibilities and probabilities based on the current odds.

19

IS TECHNICAL ANALYSIS A SELF-FULFILLING PROPHECY?

A self-fulfilling prophecy is a process whereby an original expectation creates the conditions of its own reality. With a self-fulfilling prophecy, expectations and behaviors about a future event cause the result that confirm the original prediction.

Many traders speculate that price support levels and price resistance levels have meaning because people believe they do, so they buy dips to support and sell into resistance. Technical analysis can be seen as a self-fulfilling prophecy because indicators have meaning *only* because people typically make trading decisions based on the most popular indicators. When a larger number of traders are using similar information for entry and exit decisions, it can move the price in the expected direction.

Support and resistance levels in price only have meaning if enough buyers are waiting to purchase in that price zone. A breakout in price can cause momentum traders and trend traders to buy the breakout which leads to higher prices. Many times, old resistance becomes the new support because a pullback to the breakout area allows traders that missed it the first time a second chance to get in at their desired price. Because the signal comes first and is then followed by traders, technical analysis can often be a leading indicator.

Traders should look for the most popular levels on a chart that the most traders will be watching because they find meaning there; whether it's a Fibonacci level, a key long-term moving average or an oversold level. One of the goals in technical analysis is to find the levels that the most people are waiting to react to, this will put you on the same side as the majority. Many times, price action drives more of the same behavior because it rewards one side of the market. Bull markets make the majority bullish traders, while bear markets make the majority bearish traders, and this continues as the path of least resistance until something changes sentiment.

The art and science of technical analysis is to study the patterns in market price data to identify trends and quantify the potential location of least resistance in the future. Charts can have memories because the people trading them remember their past trades. There are traders trapped in losing trades waiting to get back to even, and traders in winning trades waiting to exit at old levels of resistance. There are always traders and investors waiting to get into positions and others waiting to get out of positions, the levels they are waiting for are what creates most of technical analysis.

Stop losses and trailing stops set at key technical levels can feed on itself and cause a price to move lower. Price moving under the 200-day moving average and continuing to go lower can set off a chain reaction of multiple levels of stop losses causing a down trend to continue.

Selling creates more selling, leading to more downside momentum. The same can happen at a key profit target or resistance where sellers lock in profit and a trend ends.

When a breakout to the upside in price occurs and momentum traders and trend followers have their buy signals triggered, it creates upside momentum. Buying can create more buying as it feeds on itself, as traders with a fear of missing out rush in to chase price and short sellers are stopped out, thereby adding to the pressure. This is where swings and trends come from and why they can sometimes be short lived as the buying or selling pressure is worked through.

Is technical analysis a self-fulfilling prophecy? Yes and no. Yes, if enough people believe in the meaning of a price level or indicator signal, they will take the action that fulfills the prediction of the movement. And no, because sometimes emotions override technical analysis. It's best to think of technical analysis as a popularity contest. Only the most watched and trusted levels can affect price movement. For any technical analysis signal or reading to become popular enough to influence price action, it must be well known and acted upon.

On the flipside, sometimes technical analysis is no match for the fear or greed in the market; some people will always want in or out of a position, regardless of chart patterns. Technical analysis may be no match for one well timed tweet by an influential person or organization. News driven markets can take control of price action for a short period of time, but in the long-term, trends and indicators can still be used to create and trade robust winning systems.

Technical analysis is best used to create good risk/reward ratios in the present rather than trying to predict an unknown future. Technical analysis is your map for traveling on a chart from entry to exit. It can quantify price action, and historical price action can be your blueprint for designing a profitable trading system. Price action drives sentiment, which makes it a self-fulfilling prophecy.

20

BEYOND TECHNICAL ANALYSIS

Technical analysis is just part of successful trading. To be a profitable trader, you must bring together the important areas of trading and master them all to create a complete trading system that has an edge.

Technical analysis isn't going to make someone a successful trader unless it's incorporated into a system with a positive expectancy and quantifies a trading plan. Technical analysis is a map for understanding a chart, but profitable trading is the journey of creating wins that add up to more than losses to reach profitability.

A complete trading system includes:

- Charting
- Technical analysis
- Technical indicators
- A watchlist
- Backtesting
- Position sizing
- Risk exposure parameters
- Volatility filters

- Entry signals
- Exit signals
- Stop losses
- Trailing stops
- Profit targets
- Risk/reward ratios
- Trade journaling
- Keeping statistics
- Updating your system

Reactive technical analysis is used to build price action trading systems. A combination of price and indicators are used to create signals that quantify entries, exits, and position sizing.

When learning to develop your own trading system it is important to understand the following:

- Capital preservation should be as important to traders as capital appreciation. This avoids the risk of ruin.
- Traders should not trade any signal until after they backtested the signal for historical performance or studied historical charts for repeating patterns.
- There is a big difference between discretionary and mechanical system traders. A rule-based discretionary trader follows their rules and manages trades to minimize losses and maximize wins. Mechanical system traders follow and execute their pre-written trading plan 100% of the time. Most traders are a mixture of these two models. A discretionary trader's edge is their experience, a system trader's edge is their positive expectancy model.
- A quantified trading model with an edge will give you objectivity and consistency to trade your system, while ignoring the news or your emotions. An edge means a positive expectancy of an average win being larger than

your average loss over time. When a trader's profits are more than their losses, they make money.
- A good system will have a trader taking profits slowly but cutting losses quickly. Most profitable systems spend more time in winning traders than losing trades.
- A long-term system should eliminate much of the emotions out of any one trade through proper position sizing. A trader should be focused on the long-term performance of the next 100 trades not just the current one. Good general position sizing for most stock trading systems is no more than 10% of total capital in one trade and no greater than a 10% loss on the price of the instrument traded. These parameters would make a maximum loss be 1% of total capital on any one and keep a trader safe from the risk of ruin in almost all situations. Of course, position correlation must also be considered, and position size could be bigger with stock index ETFs and smaller if options or futures are traded, so volatility and leverage must also be considered.
- You must create a system that matches your beliefs about the markets. A trader must have faith in their system and faith in their self to trade it with discipline.
- Your system must match your tolerance for equity drawdowns and risk. Backtesting a system's equity curve is not the same as trading through losing streaks and drawdowns in real money. Most traders can only handle about half the drawdown they think they can in capital before giving up on a system or on trading itself.
- A system should be limited to a reasonable number of rules and indicators. The focus is on bigger wins than losses, not perfection. Trading is an art and a science but is more like hand grenades and horseshoes than surgery. Close enough is good enough. Filter for what matters:

good risk/reward ratios. If you wait for the perfect seat on the train it will leave without you on it.
- A trader must understand that your system will perform only when the market is conducive to that system. A trend follower will not make money in a range-bound market. A swing trader may have no signals in a strongly trending market. A buy and hold investor will not make any money in a bear market. No system or technical indicator works in all markets, it just needs to work more than it doesn't and the magnitude of the wins should be greater than the loss size over time.

A trading system will consist of what markets to trade and indicators to use for entry and exit signals. Position size should be determined based on volatility and the risk of ruin. An entry signal will open the position and the exit signal will close it; technical analysis is the best tool for creating profitable dynamics. A trader must determine a variety of exit signal possibilities whether it is a stop loss, a trailing stop, or a profit target. These are signals that should be determined by personal risk tolerance and extensive backtesting to ensure you have a robust system.

Every trade should end in one of four ways:

- A big win
- A small win
- A small loss
- Break even

Big losses should be removed as a possibility through proper position sizing and stop loss placement.

The biggest barrier to profitable trading is having large losses that destroy your capital. If you eliminate this possibility, then you have a great probability of being a profitable trader.

The most important part of any system is the trader's ability to follow it. We must understand that all trading systems have drawdowns. The odds are good that you will have ten losses in a row even with a high winning percentage. A trader must ensure they have confidence to stick with their system once they have tested it to their satisfaction and believe in its long-term profitable edge. It is dangerous to risk more than 1%-2% of total equity per trade to loss and end up blowing up an account during times when the market acts adversely to your system.

The missing piece for many traders trying to cross the bridge to profitability in the markets is combining technical analysis, position sizing, and the right mindset together to create a quantified system with an edge that they can trade with discipline over the long term.

Technical analysis is both an art and a science and your ability to find reoccurring patterns on charts improves with study and experience.

ACKNOWLEDGMENTS

Jake Wujastyk (@Trendspider_J), founding team member at TrendSpider.com used their excellent trading platform to create the historical chart images in this book. We're big fans of TrendSpider and recommend them to our students. Here are a few reasons we think their software is pretty great:

- Benzinga News Feed included (usually something that you have to buy)
- Analyst ratings
- Seasonality
- Anchored VWAP/Anchored Volume by Price
- Raindrops
- The Scanner and the Strategy Tester

A big thank you to Jake and the good folks at TrendSpider!

NEW TRADER U

Join thousands of other trading students at New Trader University! Our eCourses are created especially for those just starting out in the markets.

New Trader 101

The place to start for new traders! Become successful with less stress.

Moving Averages 101

Everything you need to know to harness the power of Moving Averages!

Price Action Trading 101

Master the concepts of reactive technical analysis and learn the best times to get in and out of your trades!

Options 101

This 19-part video course is packed with information about Options, and how they can help you up your trading game. It includes real trading examples, many visuals, and an Options Play Strategy Guide that you won't find anywhere else.

Real Trade Examples: Volume 1

Have you ever wanted to have a private consultation with Steve? To see how and why he trades the way he does? This is your chance at a fraction of the cost of a one-on-one consultation. Steve will show you step-by-step how he enters, when he exits, and the signals that he follows for maximum profitability.

Did you enjoy this eBook?

Please consider writing a review.

Listen to many of our titles on Audio!

Read more of our bestselling titles:

New Trader Rich Trader (Revised and Updated)

Moving Averages 101

So You Want to be a Trader

New Trader 101

Moving Averages 101

Buy Signals and Sell Signals

Trading Habits

Investing Habits

Calm Trader

Printed in Great Britain
by Amazon